Operation Earth Light

A GLIMPSE INTO THE
WORLD OF THE ASCENDED MASTERS

Dr. George King. A Western Master of Yoga.

Operation Earth Light

A GLIMPSE INTO THE
WORLD OF THE ASCENDED MASTERS

by
Brian C. Keneipp
Based on the original recorded transcripts of
Dr. George King
A Western Master of Yoga

The Aetherius Press
LOS ANGELES • FOUNDED 1955 • LONDON

First Published 2000

OPERATION EARTH LIGHT
A GLIMPSE INTO THE WORLD OF THE ASCENDED MASTERS

Copyright © 2000 by The Aetherius Society

ISBN No. 0-937249-17-3

Library of Congress Catalog Card No. 00-131330

Operation Earth Light—A Glimpse into the World of the Ascended Masters is printed and published by The Aetherius Press, 6202 Afton Place, Hollywood, California 90028.

*Dedicated with love and deep gratitude
to my Spiritual Master, Dr. George King*

ACKNOWLEDGEMENTS

I am indebted to Dr. George King for giving to our world Operation Earth Light and for extending to me the privilege of being involved in its beginning. I am also most grateful for his confidence in me to record this historic happening for posterity.

This book, though small in size, can be likened to an iceberg, the visible part of which is but a small part of the whole. I wish to thank the many members of The Aetherius Society, who, though unnamed here, helped indirectly and in some cases directly in Operation Earth Light and this book.

I would like to especially thank my wife Anita Keneipp, John Holder and my brother David for their invaluable help with the manuscript and Rodney Crosby for his excellent cover and book design and formatting skills.

I would also like to thank Lesley Young, Paul Nugent, Mark Keneipp, J.M. Keneipp, Richard Watson, Anita Englein, Michael Scholey, Kalan Brunink and Rodolfo Almaraz for their valuable help and support, with special thanks to Richard Lawrence for his excellent foreword and encouragement.

CONTENTS

ILLUSTRATIONS

FOREWORD

This book is a must-read work for anyone with a serious interest in metaphysics. All too often, mystical works refer back to a distant past from which they draw inspiration. Even new revelations are generally about some past teaching or event. It would be wrong to dismiss the past as irrelevant, because the greatest happenings have a timeless significance. But a modern metaphysical work does have two distinct advantages. The first one is purely practical. It is very hard to know with absolute certainty what exactly was said and done in the past because there simply was not the technology available to record it in detail. We have to rely on a combination of memory and word of mouth for much of it, which is at best unreliable.

The second advantage is even more profound. Times change and with them spiritual priorities. At the time of publication of this book, we are entering a new millennium in the Christian calendar (though many would dispute the accuracy of this date). More importantly, we are entering a New Age, known in astrological terms as the Age of Aquarius. By definition this is a time of change. The priorities have changed not only on the surface of our physical world, but even more on the highest and most spiritual realms around our planet. Operation Earth Light is undoubtedly one of the crucial aspects of this great change, and as such carries a significance that many an ancient tome, no matter how sacred, is simply not able to do.

I was privileged to be in Los Angeles, and at times in Santa Barbara, in July and August of 1990, when some of the amazing events described in this book were underway. It was staggering to witness at first hand a Master of the caliber of Dr. George King coordinating such a vast spiritual operation and, at the same time, coping with the complex business of running an international organization as versatile as The Aetherius Society. To see this from a man in his seventies was a true inspiration of what can be accomplished through a combination of phenomenal genius and sheer determination.

No one is more qualified to write this book than Brian Keneipp. He more than anyone gained an insight into the many telepathic communications Dr. King received from elevated cosmic sources in the latter part of his life. Not only did he transcribe and collate them meticulously so that they would be preserved for posterity, he also witnessed the immense physical and mental effect they had upon Dr. King. His commentaries in this book throw fascinating light upon the stresses and the joys experienced by a great Master in communion with the Gods. I must also pay tribute to him for following Dr. King's example of taking no royalties or fee for writing the book.

Many things motivated Dr. King; his love for God, his reverence for the Masters, and his immense compassion for mankind would all be at the top of the list. But he was, above all, a practical man. He knew and often stated that the most holy and sacred aspect of God with which we would come into direct physical contact is the planet upon which we live. Trained as he was in the rigorous science of yoga, which involved complete detachment from all emotion, he was unable to detach from the greatness of the Mother Earth and the foul way she has been treated by humanity. This was not a display of emotional weakness on his part; on the contrary, it was the very demonstration of his greatness. The highest part of his mission was focused on reverence for and cooperation with the Mother Earth herself. Operation Earth Light is the epitome of this reverence and cooperation at the deepest levels.

I have written an international best-selling book, but I have to say that the true measure of a book should not be the number of copies it sells. It should be its revelation of profound truth with a far-reaching significance. This book scores very highly indeed in this regard. If the reading public is wise, it will also sell a large number of copies.

Dr. Richard Lawrence
European Secretary of The Aetherius Society

AUTHOR'S PREFACE

*T*his is the story of Operation Earth Light, a mission designed to release specific frequencies of spiritual energy from the living Mother Earth out to humanity. This energy is being released gently and strategically in order to prepare mankind for the higher vibrations of a dawning New Age.

Our civilization has evolved to a critical moment in its history. From Mayan mathematicians to Nostradamus and Edgar Cayce, many prophets have predicted that great changes will occur at this time.

Many hope that the coming changes will bring in a New Age of peace and enlightenment, others fear a time of catastrophic upheaval. Even for the optimistic the trend of current events does not bode well. Materialism and greed are on the rise, while morality and compassion appear in steep decline. It is easy to imagine the predictions of doom, yet much harder to see how an enlightened New Age can manifest.

However, there are many factors unseen by mankind. Operation Earth Light is one such vital factor. Operation Earth Light was designed by Western Master of yoga, Dr. George King, in order to help guide our civilization into a New Age of peace and enlightenment and to counteract the many forces now working towards a catastrophic future.

The way Operation Earth Light came into being is an amazing story that, until now, has been known only to a handful of

Dr. King's closest disciples. I was privileged to see it develop because of my role as a disciple of Dr. King who worked tirelessly to guide the operation.

The focus of this book documents the official transfer of Operation Earth Light to the Ascended Masters in 1990. These evolved spiritual Masters have been actively guiding the evolution of mankind for thousands of years. Our knowledge of this transfer is presented in the form of recorded communications from several advanced Masters. I had the honor of taping these communications as they were received. I then transcribed the tapes for Dr. King's review and editing. Dr. King went to this trouble so that this fascinating story would be made available to all who were interested. I have added commentary to add understanding and perspective where appropriate.

In the first part of the book I reveal some of the hidden knowledge of the Ascended Masters. This is necessary in order to understand the far reaching ramifications of Operation Earth Light and to reveal its complexities and subtleties.

As the story of Operation Earth Light unfolds within these pages, the magnificent world of the Ascended Masters is revealed – a world of living planets, space travel and advanced sciences. You will meet spiritually evolved Masters of great power and advancement, yet who are very real and compassionate. You will learn how you can help bring in the New Age, for the time of sitting and watching is over and the time for action is upon us.

This book was written in order to convey a sense of hope and inspiration by revealing some of the great works now being performed by advanced Masters for the benefit of all mankind and to introduce a new and powerful way everyone can help uplift our world - the path of Karmic Healing.

Prepare yourself for a journey into the world of the Holy Ones and their concept of the Universe in which we live.

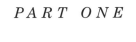

THE WORLD OF THE MASTERS

# INTRODUCTION TO PART ONE

*O*peration Earth Light is an advanced mission being performed by evolved spiritual Masters. The science and knowledge upon which this mission is based are beyond those being commonly used by mankind. I have included Part 1 of this book in order to introduce some of the concepts and sciences used by the Ascended Masters that are relevant to Operation Earth Light. Certain of these concepts you may be familiar with, while others will be new. Included are many concepts which have been revealed to humanity recently by advanced Masters, both on Earth and beyond. My purpose is to present them here so that you can understand Part 2 within the context Operation Earth Light was designed and is now being performed.

I also introduce the inventor of Operation Earth Light, Dr. George King, an unique Western Master of yoga, who was responsible for receiving many of the concepts given to humanity by the Masters. Chapter 4 contains a brief description of several of the early radionic machines Dr. King designed and built that led up to the design of Operation Earth Light.

The story of Operation Earth Light is a fascinating one, and one vital to our future. But like many great stories the scene must be set and the characters properly introduced before the story can be fully appreciated.

I introduce you now to the amazing world of the Ascended Masters.

CHAPTER 1

A NEW COSMIC PARADIGM

*T*here is one event in our history that more than any other single event defines both the time in which we now live and our future. This event is the Primary Initiation of Earth. This great cosmic happening took place on July 8th, 1964.[1] At this time the Mother Earth, an evolved, sentient Being, received colossal spiritual energy – energy that she must use to take her next step along her path of evolution.

Mankind, because of its preoccupation with materialism, did not even detect this momentous happening. That such an important spiritual happening took place on our own planet and passed us by without our notice highlights the tremendous gulf between earthman and the more evolved Masters upon other worlds. The advanced spiritual Masters knew of and were completely focused on this holy Initiation, when between 10:00 p.m. and 10:57 p.m. PDT colossal spiritual energies were manipulated into the inner core of the advanced Goddess upon which we all live. For now, this energy is being held within the Mother Earth in a state of dormancy. This is fortunate for mankind, for if she were to utilize the full potential of this energy immediately, it would so quicken the vibrations of her body that the majority of humanity could not continue to live upon her. Compassionately she has chosen to delay using this energy for as long as possible, to let a greater portion of humanity raise their vibrations to withstand this quickening when it comes.

Operation Earth Light is, effectively, a vaccine for humanity to help it prepare for the eventual full release of this energy now being held within the Mother Earth. This vaccine is being delivered very carefully in order to soften this coming release.

In their own disparate ways, many of the prophets of old foresaw this great change to our planet and our civilization. There are many upon earth today who have also realized the importance of these times. From Nostradamus to the Mayans of old and from the scientists of today to the New Age seekers – all have realized, in their own ways, the vital times in which we live. Many can feel, in one way or another, the reflection of this one great happening to our Earth, her Primary Initiation, and its impending change to our lives.

With their broader perspective, the advanced spiritual Masters on earth and other worlds see this period as a golden opportunity – a pivotal karmic moment in time! Now is a time when great manipulations on behalf of millions of humans are possible and can bring tremendous good.

These are indeed the most important days of our collective lives!

One potent way in which the Masters are helping is through world missions such as Operation Earth Light.

A New View of the Universe

Before we go on, let us stop and try to imagine the Universe as the Masters do – a Universe full of life, full of potential, full of God Itself.

Centuries ago mankind believed earth was the center of the Universe. We now know that it is not. Earth is a small planet amongst countless billions. It took mankind centuries to learn this. Whole new sciences and technologies needed to

From space, the Mother Earth begins to show the true majesty of her evolved nature.

develop in order to understand this. Yet mankind as a whole continues to believe that we are the center of the Universe in a spiritual sense.

Most people who endeavor to think and live in a spiritual way believe we learn our lessons on earth, perfect ourselves, and are then transported back to Divinity – what some call heaven, some nirvana, others absolute truth – from earth-man back to Divinity with nothing in between, never inter-acting with the rest of the Universe, as if it did not matter, as if it were not there.

In the view of the Universe held by the Masters this is not the case.

The Universe is far more magnificent. Far more logical and compassionate.

Everything is connected. Everything has a purpose. In fact, everything in the Universe is alive. The earth, the moon, the sun, the countless stars – are all alive, are advanced sen-tient conscious Beings, millions of years ahead of mankind, as mankind is millions of years ahead of the cells and atoms within us. We are all on the path back to Divinity, though we are, even now, a part of Divinity.

Once we master our lessons on earth we can leave the cycle of rebirth by constructing a more subtle and long-last-ing body. At this point, called ascension, some choose to remain on earth to help their "underclassmen." They become part of the Spiritual Hierarchy of Earth also known as the Great White Brotherhood (all references to "white" herein have nothing to do with race but with a high frequency of subtle energy). This ancient brotherhood is composed of Ascended Masters from all races and religions and consists of both females and males. They work tirelessly to bring peace and enlightenment to humanity. These are the beings who are now performing Operation Earth Light. Other "gradu-ates" from the school known as Earth, choose to move on to other planets within this solar system, living within other realms and dimensions. These advanced beings, now known as Cosmic Masters, begin helping others throughout the galaxy to evolve.

This pattern continues for millions of years. At some point in the distant future we merge with other life streams to become greater and more evolved beings as we continue our journey back to Divinity.[2]

At every stage we are conscious, sentient, and alive.

THIS is the view of the Universe held by the Masters. This is the Cosmic Concept.

There are many aspects of this view of the Universe that are not new to humanity.

Most of the ancient races - the indigenous peoples - worshiped the Sun and the Earth as advanced aspects of God. They knew instinctively what most modern men and women have forgotten. The Sun and the Earth are not here by chance, by some fluke of nature. They are advanced sentient Beings who help mankind and countless other life streams by providing the energy and materials for our current experiences, so that we can evolve into greater and greater beings within Creation.

This expanded view of the Universe has been given to mankind during the last half of the 20th century by the Cosmic Masters. It is far from the first time we have received wisdom from such evolved sources. The teachings of Krishna, Buddha, Jesus, and many others, also came directly from advanced civilizations in order to help mankind live by the Divine laws. This new cosmic paradigm has been given now to enhance our existing teachings, not to replace them. It seeks to bring the spiritual teachings of the past into the age of science and space exploration and to prepare mankind for its next step in evolution towards God, a preparation for the coming New Age.

This is our path, this is the Universe in which we live. One of the keys to this new paradigm is the continuity of consciousness and the taking of greater responsibility for our own evolution. We are being helped. But we must learn what the Masters learned long ago. They have learned that the greatest actions are those done in service to others. They spend their whole lives providing assistance and energy to lower life forms. They have learned through time that all is indeed One.

With this expanded concept as our guide I will go over briefly some other spiritual concepts needed to understand Operation Earth Light. Most of these, such as karma and reincarnation, have been known on earth for centuries; however, when looked at in the light of the Cosmic Concept they will become clearer.

Karma

Karma is the great law of God; in fact, it is part of God Itself. It is through the workings of this law that the different aspects of the Absolute move back to their source through time and experience. Lord Buddha described karma as, "Action and reaction are opposite and equal." The Master Jesus taught the same law in different words: "As you sow, so shall you reap." Simply put in modern terms, what you give out you receive back.

Send out selfishness and negativity and one gets this back, until such a time that one learns to act otherwise. Send out love and healing, and one gets these energies back.

The effect of this law, which applies to every aspect of Creation, is to teach one to move back towards God. It is, in the words of Dr. King, "pressure towards conformity." Much has been written on this subject over the centuries. The more evolved beings study this all-pervasive law and use it in all their actions. It is central to many of the advanced world missions being performed for mankind, including Operation Earth Light.

At this unique point in our history the pressures of karma on earth are reaching an all-time high. This is due to the karmic pressure of the Mother Earth to evolve, to use the energies that she was given in 1964. Yet much of humanity is not ready for this heightened vibration. The Masters are doing what they can to speed up mankind's journey through karma. It is up to all of us to do our part as well.

Reincarnation

Reincarnation is the process whereby a given consciousness can learn and evolve using different bodies through an extended time period. The journey back to the Absolute will take billions of years. Just to master the lessons available in an earth body can take thousands or even millions of years. Yet the current earth body can only last about 100 years. Reincarnation is a way to continue one's lessons through numerous human forms, until the lessons available on earth have been mastered.

We must not take for granted the part a planet plays in our lives. At this point in our evolution we need a planet to live on to protect us from the rigors of space. We need a planet on which to reincarnate and material with which to create for ourselves a body to experience life through. The Mother Earth has provided such a haven for us for millions of years.

Other Realms

The prospect of raising the consciousness of the six billion people on earth, or at least as many as possible, before the great change is indeed a daunting thought. Yet there are actually many more souls upon earth than those on the physical plane.

In between lives an individual inhabits the other realms.

These realms have been written about for centuries – heaven and hell to the Christian, and Lokas to the Buddhist. Following the death of the body, the consciousness inhabits a more subtle body. This subtle body is a part of one's aura while still living in a physical body on the physical realm. The subtle body is still physical, yet of a quicker vibration than the physical body. Once the physical body dies the consciousness is housed solely in the subtle body. At this time the individual begins to live on the other realms of earth. He will interact with others on those realms. It is possible that certain very sensitive people on the physical realm who are sufficiently clairvoyant can contact him. However, the connection to the physical realm is largely severed for a number of years. During this time the individual continues to grow and learn. The personality is retained. He will remember life on the physical plane and will recognize friends and relatives from his physical life whom he meets on the other realms. The individual's lessons are different on the other realms yet are still molded by his karmic pattern. There are many realms around earth. Some of these realms are similar to the physical realms, others dark and rough, known as the lower realms or the hells, and others very spiritual and uplifting, known as the higher realms or heavens. The karmic pattern created by the sum total of one's thoughts and actions will determine which realm one goes to at death.

Then, when the time is right and according to one's karma, the individual is reborn onto the physical realm into another life of essential experiences. These experiences are specially prepared to help the individual to learn the lessons needed to evolve beyond his existence in an earth body.

Other Worlds

The final initiation on earth is known as ascension. Once a life stream passes through this portal, he chooses one of two courses of action. He can either remain on earth as a member of the Great White Brotherhood and help mankind or he can proceed to a higher classroom in a more evolved civilization. These higher classrooms exist on other planets in our solar system and beyond, and exist on higher realms. As the beings upon these planets, known as Cosmic Masters, have evolved past the need for rebirths, they are able to exist on any one of the levels of vibration, or other realms, in their physical bodies. They choose the higher realms because it is easier to invoke and manipulate the higher energies there.

Because the beings upon the other planets are more evolved, these planets, unlike Earth, were able to pass through their initiations and heighten their vibrations without harming those living upon them. In fact, when the inhabitants are sufficiently advanced themselves, the quickened vibrations of the planet can be of great benefit to the inhabitants.

On these advanced worlds the individual continues his study of karma, the manipulation of spiritual energy, and the advanced sciences. He learns how to help other lesser-evolved beings or civilizations evolve. This type of study and growth continues through several levels of planetary existence and lasts for millions of years, for one still has a long way to go. Most of our religious founders have been Cosmic Masters from other worlds who have come to earth, taking on an earth body for a life, bringing to our civilization essential teachings of the laws of God. Shri Krishna, Lord Buddha, and the Master Jesus were three such beings. There were others as well. The three examples I have mentioned took on earth bodies in order to manipulate our karmic pattern. Most often the advanced beings from other planets come and do their works unseen by man. This is due to the necessities of our rather difficult karmic pattern.

Such interplanetary visitors to earth have increased at

this time because of the impending changes and humanity's great need during this transitional period. Several of these Cosmic Masters were closely involved in the construction of the Operation Earth Light equipment, and their communications with Dr. King appear later in this book.

The Great White Brotherhood

The other course of action available for the earthman who passes through the portal of ascension is to become a member of the Spiritual Hierarchy of Earth, also known as the Great White Brotherhood. These advanced Masters have decided to stay back on earth rather than progress on to higher civilizations in order to more actively help mankind evolve through missions such as Operation Earth Light. These highly evolved spiritual beings sacrifice greatly to stay and help their lesser-evolved brothers. Much has been written about the Great White Brotherhood over the centuries. Not all of it is accurate, in part because they have been limited by how openly they could work due to mankind's negative karmic pattern. This will be discussed in more detail in Chapter 3. These advanced beings currently live beneath large mountains in hollowed-out structures called retreats. Some of these retreats have become well known, and strange phenomena have been seen in their vicinity. Such places as the Andes, the Himalayas, the Tetons, Luxor, Mount Shasta and Mount Kilimanjaro are amongst the best known. It was to two of these centers that Dr. King visited in a projected state to observe the early prototypes of the Operation Earth Light equipment.

The Earth

The Earth has long been revered by the indigenous peoples all over the world. Even the scientists of today are ready to believe that the Earth truly is a living, breathing entity.

Another cycle comes to a close. Through the centuries the scientific and logical minds that took mankind away from this reverence for our home planet are now returning to this elevated thought. The resurgence of this innate belief in a living, compassionate Mother Earth is just the beginning of a true appreciation of the vastness of this holy Being.

After millions of lives evolving through the experiences afforded on the more advanced planets, a life stream slowly starts to merge with other similarly evolved beings. Eventually, this combined entity is born as a planet. This is but another step along the road back to the Absolute Itself.

When one begins to realize that the Mother Earth is indeed a sentient and holy Being many thoughts crystallize in one's mind. We owe a tremendous debt to this Being. She gives us sustenance. She gives us a home in the midst of cold, empty space – a home suitable for gaining experience at our current level of evolution.

Knowing that she has been given tremendous energies which she can use to rise to her next level of existence and that she is holding up the use of this energy for as long as possible – for our benefit – is truly the key to understanding the coming New Age and our place in it.

The Masters know this and are working hard to help mankind evolve quickly, so that the Mother Earth can take her rightful place in the heavens with as much of humanity as possible being able to remain on her.

The Sun and Beyond

The Mother Earth, as great and evolved as she is, is still a long way from the end of the path. These are the awe-inspiring thoughts contained within the Cosmic Concept. Everything is alive, sentient, and evolving. The sun, the double stars, the nebulas, the comets, the galaxies, the galactic systems – it goes on and on and on. The black holes, the neutron stars, the quasars – are all alive, are all evolving back towards the Absolute, are all part of the Absolute, are all connected.

This cosmic paradigm opens up tremendous new vistas of thought for it allows one to live and experience life more fully, more completely.

We can walk outside on a warm summer night and observe the crescent moon conjunct to a bright and sparkling Venus. Our mind can then expand to dwell upon the vastness of the Universe, the vastness of the Absolute, and to remember that we are indeed a part of the magnificent whole. In fact, one day we will visit distant planets, learning through fantastic experiences and helping others less evolved than ourselves. Indeed, one day we will even become a part of such evolved Beings.

CHAPTER 2

WHO IS DR. GEORGE KING REALLY?

*T*he unique times in which we live demanded a unique person to help bridge the gap between our spiritually backward civilization and the coming New Age of enlightenment. The new message of the Cosmic Concept required a messenger of outstanding and rare abilities. The urgency of these days demanded a strong man capable of spiritual action, capable of developing karmic missions such as Operation Earth Light. The one chosen by the Masters was Dr. George King.

Dr. King was contacted by Cosmic Masters in 1954. At that time Dr. King, at the age of 35, had already achieved mastery over his physical and mental body through years of advanced yoga practice and was by then a master of yoga. As such, he was capable of a very high degree of mind control only dreamed about by most. At the time of his initial contact Dr. King was using his special abilities to develop different types of radionic healing devices. One device used the healing power of color applied to physical pills and another device was designed to extract the healing essence from pharmaceutical drugs and apply this essence to the body, thereby avoiding unwanted side effects. He was collaborating psychically with certain advanced scientists residing on the higher realms, such as Sir James Young Simpson, a Scottish pioneer in the development of ether,

Dr. King on Mount Ramshead, Australia, during the worldwide mission, Operation Starlight, 1960.

and Sir Oliver Lodge, a renowned physicist instrumental in the development of the radio.

The Cosmic Masters are advanced beings capable of many advanced feats. One such feat is the ability to see the karmic pattern of individuals. They can read one's past lives or even future lives as clearly as a book. They knew that Dr. King was capable of bringing their message to earth in these days and of helping actively in their goal of uplifting mankind. In all likelihood, the Cosmic Masters also had a hand in arranging his development in past lives.

The messages of the Cosmic Masters had to be delivered in a very exacting manner, without any dilution. As a master of yoga, Dr. King could control his mind to a sufficiently high degree to do this. He was able to bring about a state of consciousness known as a samadhic trance state – a state that has been used through the ages by the great eastern Masters to uncover the ancient truths.

Shortly after Dr. King's first contact by the Cosmic Masters, he was approached by an advanced Master from India living in an earth body. He taught Dr. King how to modify the samadhic trance state into a state specially designed to receive the messages of the Cosmic Masters in a very pure form.

Dr. King realized the importance of this call and immediately stopped his advanced medical research and devoted all of his time to aid the Cosmic Masters help our world.

The messages, or "transmissions," from the Cosmic Masters started in earnest in 1955. These transmissions covered hundreds of different subjects, varying from the dangers of atomic experimentation and mankind's spiritual development to advanced cosmic philosophy.

In order to prepare for the essential tasks ahead, the Cosmic Masters ordered Dr. King to form a new organization. To give this organization a correct start, a member of the

Great White Brotherhood from beneath Mount Shasta visualized it into existence. It was named The Aetherius Society, based on the pseudonym of the first Cosmic Master to transmit information through Dr. King, the Master Aetherius.

By this time Dr. King had come a long way from his simple beginnings in Shropshire, England, where he was born on January 23rd, 1919. Yet his new life was only just beginning for he was destined for missions as yet undreamed of.

The World Missions Commence

Almost simultaneously, two great Missions were handed to Dr. King in July of 1958. He was given the tremendous responsibility of serving as the mental channel through whom the advanced Master we knew as Jesus delivered *The Twelve Blessings*. This sacred text was an extension of his Sermon on the Mount and included a new Cosmic Concept. At the same time Dr. King began the titanic job of performing Operation Starlight. In this mission he climbed 18 mountains around the world chosen by the Cosmic Masters. Once at the chosen spot, the Cosmic Masters sent an initial charge of spiritual energy through him into the mountain. The Masters would complete the charge at a later time, making each mountain a holy place where others could climb and tap into a tremendous storehouse of spiritual energy and send it out to the world. So potent are these holy mountains that an ordinary person can send out as much spiritual energy as an advanced adept.[3]

The Missions Evolve

Dr. King soon learned that his major tasks on earth involved devising missions so that mankind could cooperate with the Masters in these critical days to heal and uplift our world. The Masters of the Great White Brotherhood and the Cosmic Masters are working in many ways to help mankind evolve.

However, due to the law of karma, they can best help mankind by helping mankind help itself. In Dr. King they had an exceptional individual trained through the discipline of yoga and well-versed in radionics and metaphysics. As such he was capable of designing and performing powerful karmic missions for earth.

Dr. King needed to invent several radionic machines in order to perform these advanced world missions. Machines were designed to receive, store, and transmit spiritual energy. This took an unique blend of knowledge, determination and sheer hard work. He had to create the machines from scratch, as there was little usable knowledge on earth of much help. These machines formed the important groundwork for the Operation Earth Light equipment and will be discussed in more detail in Chapter 4.

During this time Dr. King developed a close working relationship with the Great White Brotherhood and certain Cosmic Masters. He had demonstrated his complete dedication to helping and healing mankind. In return, these advanced beings were allowed to help on many occasions. They gave advice in the building of certain radionic machines, provided clues in the discovery of psychic centers of Earth and even manipulated spiritual energy through the radionic machines out to the world; all to uplift and heal our backward world.

In the years that I was a close personal disciple of Dr. King, I witnessed hundreds of transmissions between Dr. King and many different Cosmic Masters and members of the Great White Brotherhood. There was tremendous love and mutual respect between Dr. King and the advanced beings. They were pleased at the tremendous good he and The Aetherius Society were doing through the missions he developed. Dr. King sacrificed all for God and was working 24 hours a day to help our world, as were the Masters themselves.

The relationship between Dr. King and the Cosmic Masters during the later years of his life was not solely one of disciple to Master. Although Dr. King revered the Cosmic Masters as many lives more evolved than he, Dr. King functioned more as an advanced field agent on earth. He could understand mankind, as one of them, yet he also understood the science of radionics and energy manipulation used by the Cosmic Masters. Because of his position on earth, he was able to perform missions for mankind that the Cosmic Masters were not able to perform due to karmic restrictions. Dr. King was virtually a karmic agent on earth for the Cosmic Masters.

The Missions were the main focus of attention of both Dr. King and The Aetherius Society for the rest of his life. They were and are essential for our world and have helped tremendously over the years, as a brief review of modern history from the time of the contact in May 1954 to the present day will uncover. The urgency and seriousness of these missions and the advanced nature of the messages from the Cosmic Masters made it difficult to share Dr. King's work with the public properly. Nevertheless, acclaim has found him. To mention just one of his numerous honors: on July 19th, 1981 Dr. King received the Prize of Peace and Justice from the International Union of Christian Chivalry for his tireless work and charity to humanity. Previous Peace and Justice prizes have been awarded to Professor Albert Einstein, Mother Teresa, Dr. Henry Kissinger and Dr. Albert Schweitzer.

Considering the amazing abilities and accomplishments of Dr. King, many have pushed for further details of his past and a further explanation of his abilities. Dr. King himself never came out publicly and stated that he was anything other than an earth Master. He preferred to let the results of his life speak for themselves. It is clear, however, to all who knew him that there was much more to Dr. King than was publicly stated. For the purpose of this book, I prefer to follow Dr. King's lead and state simply that he was an advanced Master in an earth body, closely associated with the Spiritual Hierarchy of Earth, known as the Great White Brotherhood. If you would like to study his life in more depth I would encourage you to do so through the bibliography.

Dr. King passed on from his physical structure on earth on July 12th, 1997. His world-saving missions – including Operation Earth Light and his spiritual brotherhood, The Aetherius Society – continue his unique legacy to our world.

CHAPTER 3

Yesterday, Today and Tomorrow

*I*n Chapter 1, I just touched the surface of the ocean of knowledge within the Cosmic Concept. To understand Operation Earth Light we must delve deeper, including how our civilization arrived at its current predicament.

The Dark History of Mankind

Over 18,000,000 years ago, mankind lived on another planet called Maldek, within this solar system. We had attained a level of science and evolution somewhat beyond where we are today. At that time we also had discovered the power of the atom; in fact we were even more adept at its use. Through a worldwide war we released so much power from our weapons that we committed the horrendous crime of destroying our planet. All that remains is the asteroid belt. If you try and imagine the karma associated with such an act you can start to understand the difficulty of our current situation.

Mankind needed a place to continue its evolution and to start again to learn its essential lessons. The Mother Earth was approached and asked if she would allow our incarnation upon her back in order to give us a home. She agreed. Such an advanced Being as a planet would know, to a very great degree, what she was getting herself into. Her acceptance was truly an act of Godly compassion.

Throughout the centuries mankind slowly evolved once again and another civilization grew. Some metaphysicians know of this civilization as Lemuria. This civilization also succumbed to the attraction of the atom. We again destroyed ourselves; only this time with less power and did not destroy the planet. Another period of evolution followed, culminating in the civilization of Atlantis. Once again we fell into the same trap, developing atomic weapons. Once again we destroyed our civilization.

Truth is often stranger than fiction. There is now a growing body of evidence that more and more points to these facts, from the legends of the ancient Hindu texts to the theories by modern astronomers that the asteroid belt is the result of a planet destroyed through a massive explosion.[4]

With this encapsulation of our 18,000,000-year history on earth, one can better understand just how much the Mother Earth has had to hold back her development in order to sustain us.

There are great cosmic resources being applied to our world to reverse the downward slide of our civilization. The time to act is now. The Cosmic Masters have learned that the most powerful way to change this tide is through the advanced science of positive karmic manipulation.

The Manipulation of Karma

There is a compassionate pole to the impersonal pressure of karma. This pole allows for the manipulation of karma providing one can understand how to do this.

Every action by the Cosmic Masters is designed to bring about the greatest karmic good for as many people as possible. Most of the work of Dr. King on earth was to improve the karma of mankind.

The manipulation of karma is a very advanced subject and one in which I have much to learn. However, I was fortunate to have lived and worked very closely with Dr. King, who was a master of the positive manipulation of karma. I will attempt to explain some of what I learned on this subject – a subject that is essential to the future of mankind on earth.

In the words of Dr. King, "Karma is pressure towards conformity. It is pressure directing you, the mind and you, the soul toward you, the Spirit."

It is first important to understand that karma is a pressure, a force. It is not a punishment or reward system developed by a benevolent or wrathful personal God. It is a force that follows certain laws that can be manipulated. The purpose of the force is to move a life stream back toward God.

A good example of the manipulation of an individual's karma was illustrated in the film *Ghandi*, the life story of Mahatma Ghandi. At a time during riots in India between the Muslims and the Hindus, a Hindu man approached Ghandi and confessed to the crime of killing a Muslim boy during a riot and asked what he could do to atone for this crime. Ghandi advised the man to adopt a Muslim boy of about the same age whose father had been killed during the riots. He should then raise him as his own son and as a Muslim not a Hindu.

The karma caused by killing a boy during a state of rage would tend to cause the reaction of being killed himself in a future life under similar circumstances. This would teach through experience the mistake of killing. The pressure of karma would tend to bring this experience. However, this man could relieve the pressure of the karma he caused by learning the lesson before the pressure forced the lesson. By adopting a Muslim boy of the same age as the one he killed and raising him as his own son, the man would learn many things. He would learn the value of a life by raising such a boy, for he would always remember the boy he had killed each time he looked at his adopted son. He would learn also the positive aspects of the Islamic religion by helping the boy grow up as a Muslim. His misunderstanding of Islam caused his rage, and his lack of appreciation of the preciousness of life allowed him to kill. By taking upon himself the experience necessary to learn these lessons himself he could relieve the pressure of karma. He would thus be manipulating his karma.

Just as individuals have karma, so do groups of individuals, countries, and mankind as a whole. This is an even more advanced area of study than individual karma.

World Karma

A dictator in a third world country committing terrible atrocities will, of course, bring the pressure of karma to bear on himself and all who carry out his orders. However, everyone on earth is also partly responsible. Many know about his evil acts yet do not take action, whatever that may be, to stop it. And even those who do not know consciously about these actions are also partly responsible, as the higher part of the individual does know. We are, as we have been told many times in the past, our brother's keeper. The pressure of karma will continue to work to get this message into us, until it is well rooted. On the positive side, as a member of mankind does good work for others, this too is reckoned in our worldwide karma. As a part of our group soul acts, we are all affected. In fact one of the greatest actions that a member of the Great White Brotherhood performs is to stay back on earth to help mankind. Since he is still a member of mankind, this therefore helps raise the karma of all mankind.

A positive karmic pattern for a group will help an individual within that group learn his own karmic lessons by providing a more conducive environment. Logically the greater the act performed for mankind the greater the positive karmic manipulation.

One of the great benefits of Operation Earth Light is in

its positive manipulation of world karma. On a practical level it releases some of the initiatory energies now held within the Mother Earth. This release helps to speed up her evolution. As Operation Earth Light was designed by Dr. King, a Master in an earth body, and is being performed by members of the Great White Brotherhood, it helps mankind's overall karma. It demonstrates that mankind, as represented by Dr. King and the Great White Brotherhood, are concerned enough about the Mother Earth to work in this way for her benefit.

Service – The Key to Evolution in these Days

During these pivotal days, it is up to everyone on earth to help evolve our race. Service is by far the greatest act that can be performed by anyone.

The message of service to others is a keynote of the communications coming from the Cosmic Masters.

For centuries the more advanced systems of religion taught that the highest stage of evolution on earth came from detaching oneself from civilization in order to achieve the higher states. This is no longer the case. It is still true that in order to go through the initiation of ascension one must spend time alone in controlling one's mind. However, at this time in our history it is imperative that all spiritually-minded individuals work for the greater good – work to help as many people as possible raise themselves so that they may be able to withstand the coming change on earth.

Service has always been an essential lesson upon the path back to God and was clearly taught in all the major religions. Now it is an essential action for all upon the path, no matter what level of advancement they have obtained.

Spiritual Energy

One way that everyone can help others rise and grow is to

send out to them a stream of uplifting spiritual energy through prayer and healing. Unfortunately, there is much confusion as to what exactly spiritual energy is and how it can be tapped into and used.

Spiritual energy is a form of subtle energy not well known to scientists on earth. The Chi or Ki of Chinese acupuncture is a form of this subtle energy. The seemingly miraculous capabilities of psychics are a result of their ability to detect this subtle energy. There are many frequencies of this energy. The higher frequencies are uplifting and healing and helpful, while the lower frequencies, such as those frequencies used in voodoo or black magic rituals, can be damaging and hurtful.

Just as our current civilization uses electricity, magnetism, and electromagnetic waves, the more advanced civilizations use and manipulate spiritual energy. These subtle forms of energy abide by certain laws of nature, just as electromagnetism abides by certain laws. Spiritual energy can be manipulated by concentrated thought, which is how prayer and spiritual healing work. There is a sea of this energy all around us. The ancient yoga masters called this energy Prana, the main source of which, in our system, is the Sun. The mind, with sufficient concentration, can focus this energy and direct it to a specific destination. If one prays for world peace, for example, this energy is first accumulated within our aura from the Sun through the atmosphere. It is then conditioned by our concentrated thought and given a direction to create peace on our world. Unfortunately, most on earth are not well versed in the use and control of spiritual energy. There are, however, many techniques and practices that can be learned by one seeking to become more proficient in this, as fortunately there is now a greater desire to learn such methods than ever before.[5]

Spiritual energy can also be focused and manipulated

using machines. The fledgling sciences of radionics and shape power do just that. On the more advanced planets these sciences are very evolved. One example of shape power on earth is the Great Pyramid of Giza. In world missions performed by the Great White Brotherhood and The Aetherius Society, such as Operation Earth Light and Operation Sunbeam, the spiritual energy manipulated is so great and the destination so focused that radionic equipment must be used.

Spiritual Pushes

Just as there is a wide range of frequencies within the electromagnetic spectrum, so there is also a wide range of frequencies within the subtle energy spectrum. As a person progresses through evolution, he attunes himself more and more to these subtle energies. This energy can give him greater power that can be used for either good or evil. Mankind used this energy for more basic and materialistic tendencies on the planet Maldek and later during the civilizations of Lemuria and Atlantis. This demonstrated a lack of reverence for the higher energies. One part of the karmic ramifications from our destruction of Maldek was the creation of a certain aspect of the ionosphere. This portion of the atmosphere filters subtle energy making it more difficult to attract. Following our self-destruction in the days of Lemuria and Atlantis this portion of the ionosphere was intensified. One of mankind's vital lessons is to learn to use the subtle energies with reverence and to help and uplift itself and others.

One of the first actions taken by the Cosmic Masters in these modern days was to make the higher aspects of this subtle energy more available to mankind. On May 28th, 1958, the first known Spiritual Push, also known as Magnetization Period, took place. These Spiritual Pushes have continued every year to date and will continue into the future. During these times a large spacecraft known as

Dr. King manipulates spiritual energy into a radionic bat-
tery during Operation Prayer Power, held on the side of Lake
Powell, Utah.

Satellite No. 3 comes into orbit of earth. This craft remains invisible in order to avoid unwanted panic by the military. It has very advanced radionic instrumentation onboard capable of detecting the thought and actions of all upon earth and the movement of subtle energies. As individuals or groups of individuals attempt to use and send out the higher octaves of subtle energy called spiritual energy, this craft magnifies the energy available to them. During these Spiritual Pushes the Cosmic Masters virtually take energy from the Sun (energy that would normally be filtered by the ionosphere due to mankind's past karma) and transmit this energy directly to those who would use such energy in selfless and uplifting ways. It is truly one of the great karmic manipulations of our time. As one learns to use this energy more and more, one is also helping others to become more attuned to such energies as well by increasing its flow throughout our world.

The Devic Kingdom
The Devic Kingdom is another group of living beings on earth who constitute a very important factor to the deeper understanding of Operation Earth Light. These beings are known to some as the nature forces and consist of many different types of entities. They are physical beings living on earth, yet they exist on a different vibratory plane. Some of the more commonly known types of lesser devas are the fairies and gnomes often seen in nature by children and clairvoyants. The Devic Kingdom is responsible for the transference of subtle energies into physical manifestation upon earth. Using the energies given to them by the Mother Earth, humanity and other sources the devas create the weather and other "natural processes" on earth. This is done strictly according to certain laws. They must utilize all the energies invoked on earth. Therefore, the thoughts and energies radiated by mankind directly influence the weather and other biological

and geological processes. There are no accidents in the, so-called, acts of God such as droughts, hurricanes and earth-quakes. The devas are impartial and must use the energy given to them. If they receive negative, discordant energies they must use this energy as well.

On a more positive note, the devas are also responsible for transferring mankind's prayers into actualized results. If one were to invoke a prayer for the healing of a certain person, for example, this spiritual energy would be delivered by devic forces to the aura of that person for him or her to use. The greater the concentration of mind and heart put behind such a prayer, the greater will be the energy delivered by the devas to the destination. Exactly how this is accomplished is an important study but is outside the scope of this book.

The Devic Kingdom has a very important role to play in the coming changes on earth. It will be instrumental in trans-lating and incorporating the higher energy vibrations from the Initiation of the Mother Earth into actual physical mani-festation. The devas will respond to the release of this great and beautiful energy and will change the weather; will change the geology and the biology of earth to a thing of even greater wonder than it is now. These holy energies – released through Operation Earth Light – will go directly to the Devic Kingdom for it to use in this monumental task.

The World Operations of the Masters

After being contacted by the Cosmic Masters, Dr. King spent his life finding new ways that he and his organization, The Aetherius Society, could help mankind evolve. He quickly learned that the most efficient and powerful means to help our civilization is through powerful worldwide karmic manipulations. He called these operations Cosmic Missions. Operation Earth Light, the subject of this book, was one such mission. Most of the other missions designed by Dr. King are still being performed by The Aetherius Society. Four of the most important of these are Operation Starlight, Operation Sunbeam, Operation Prayer Power and The Saturn Mission.

Operation Starlight

Dr. King's first mission, Operation Starlight, was given to him in 1958 by the Cosmic Masters. It took over three years to perform and was an essential forerunner of several missions to follow. In Operation Starlight Dr. King climbed 18 mountains around the world and acted as a channel through which tremendous spiritual energy was sent into each mountain. These mountains were charged in order to give mankind another means to tap into the spiritual energy that has become more difficult for him to contact due to his karmic pattern. These 18 mountains, plus an additional one that was charged in another way, are now virtually spiritual energy batteries. Unlike electrical batteries, these batteries cannot be discharged; in fact, for certain metaphysical reasons, the more they are used the more powerful they become. Theoretically, the Cosmic Masters could have charged all these mountains with spiritual energy without the presence of Dr. King. However, as a member of mankind, Dr. King manipulated the karma of mankind through his physical effort of climbing the mountains and using his advanced abilities to achieve the elevated yogic trance-state that allowed the energy to flow through him. Remember that any act done by a part of the whole reflects back onto the whole. The physical effort of Dr. King and the teams that helped him manipulated part of the karma to allow these mountains to be charged.

These holy mountains are now available to all who wish to climb them and send out uplifting spiritual energy to the world.[6]

Operation Sunbeam

Operation Sunbeam is one of the most effective karmic manipulations now being performed on earth. In this mission, Dr. King again drew upon his knowledge of the divinity of the Mother Earth and his experience with the science of radionics and the law of karma.

The modus operandi for Operation Sunbeam is to take spiritual energy earmarked for mankind and give it to the Mother Earth instead.

The logic of this mission is that the energy put into the 19 holy mountains in Operation Starlight by the Cosmic Masters was put there for mankind's use. The energy is available to mankind, and is sealed off from Earth herself. Dr. King designed and built radionic equipment to collect and store the energy from the mountains so that it could be released in a highly concentrated form to the Mother Earth.

Several psychic centers of the Mother Earth were discovered and researched by Dr. King in order to determine how to transmit the collected power from the holy mountains through these centers into the Mother Earth. Just as the human body has psychic centers which receive and transmit subtle energies so does the body of the Mother Earth.

After years of work and effort the first units of energy were transmitted to the Mother Earth on September 24th, 1966. Since that time there have been many improvements made, and the mission continues today.

Although the amount of energy given to the Mother Earth is very small compared to what she uses, it is the gesture or token repayment that is important. It has become an essential karmic manipulation on behalf of mankind. Most of mankind continues to deplete earth's resources in a selfish and uncaring fashion, not even aware that she is an evolved, living, feeling entity. When a portion of mankind offers spiritual energy to the Mother Earth, energy that was meant for mankind, a powerful manipulation of the karma of mankind as a whole takes place.

Operation Prayer Power

The spiritual energy of prayer is one of the greatest healing forces available to mankind. It can be used to heal individuals and groups alike. It is truly the power of Love in action. Prayer has been taught throughout the ages, and it forms an essential part of all major religions. Millions of people throughout the world regularly use this form of energy and help the world more than they may realize. When an earthquake or other such catastrophe occurs on earth, millions of spiritually minded people send their prayers to help those in need. This is like gentle rain falling upon an uncontrolled fire. The more who join in prayer, the harder the rain falls. Imagine if one could harness the rain, collect it together and pour it in a flowing stream onto such a raging fire of suffering. The effects would be multiplied exponentially. Dr. King's mission Operation Prayer Power does just this.

Dr. King was able to modify the radionic equipment he invented for Operation Sunbeam and use it for Operation Prayer Power.

Each week spiritually-minded people join together at centers around the world for Operation Prayer Power charging sessions. Using dynamic prayer, eastern mantra and mystic mudras, tremendous prayer energy is invoked. This is collected and stored in a radionic battery set up in the middle of the room. These charging sessions continue week after week, filling each battery with thousands of prayer hours of spiritual energy. (The amount of spiritual energy invoked by one person praying with full concentration for one hour is termed one prayer hour.)

Wherever there is a crisis on earth, such as a hurricane,

earthquake or war, this storehouse of uplifting energy can be released almost immediately through a machine known as a Spiritual Energy Radiator. This radionic device can discharge a spiritual battery in a fraction of the time it takes to charge it. This river of spiritual energy is then distributed by cooperating Masters to the area in need. In this mission the Devic Kingdom is often bypassed by the Masters to ensure a quicker result.

Since this world mission started in 1973, Dr. King and The Aetherius Society have had astounding successes aiding victims of catastrophes and other "natural" disasters.[7]

Operation Prayer Power energy can be used in many of the same ways that normal prayer can be used – to try to create peace in the face of an impending war, to offset world karma that is about to cause a catastrophic hurricane, or to ease the pain and suffering following an earthquake or flood.

The Saturn Mission

The Saturn Mission will be discussed in Chapter 4.

 A World Mission Evolves

*R*adionic machines, as well as the human mind, can manipulate spiritual energy. As stated in the last Chapter, there are many occasions when a radionic device is needed, especially when spiritual energy is being manipulated on a global scale. Dr. King realized the importance of such machines early on. However, there was very little research to draw upon on earth at the time. He virtually had to start from the beginning through painstaking trial and error. With his well-developed mental abilities he was first able to construct certain of these machines on the other realms through concentrated visualization. He could then watch them work and make minor adjustments prior to having them constructed by Aetherius Society technicians on the physical plane.

The first radionic device was composed of two machines, lovingly named Gertie and Gertina by the operators. One of them was built based upon a mental impression given to Dr. King by the Masters in the late 1950s. In a later transmission received on April 22nd, 1959, the Master Aetherius gave details of how to potentize this device. It was first used in cooperation with Satellite No. 3 during a Spiritual Push starting on November 18th, 1959. In the beginning it was used as a type of safety valve in conjunction with the regular power circles held at the London Headquarters during every Spiritual Push in those days. These power circles consisted of people joining together in prayer and mantra. Spiritual energy was sent through them by the controllers onboard Satellite No. 3. This energy would often accumulate in the local vicinity and cause a condition known as "resonance." Although it is positive uplifting energy, at a certain level of saturation the energy starts to reflect upon itself, thereby causing a detrimental effect. The radionic instrument acted as a pressure valve to relieve this situation. It was soon discovered that this instrument could also transmit the spiritual energy coming directly from Satellite No. 3 without going through human channels. It did not replace the power circles, which continue to this day, but became another way to send out spiritual energy. Since the machine was designed, built, and operated by humans, it was also another way to improve the karmic pattern of mankind.

Shortly after, another radionic machine was designed by Dr. King. This machine was built at The Aetherius Society headquarters in Los Angeles for an operation performed off the coast of Newport Beach, California, called Operation Bluewater.[8] After the completion of this mission, this radionic machine was also used to send out energy from Satellite No. 3 during Spiritual Pushes. By 1965, Dr. King was already providing two radionic machines for use by the Cosmic Masters during their Spiritual Pushes, yet this was just the beginning.

Dr. King's Mission Evolves

How Operation Earth Light and the equipment for this mission evolved from these first two machines is an interesting history and illustrates how necessary it is for even the Cosmic Masters to modify their plans as conditions change.

Less than one year after the Primary Initiation of Earth, on March 15th, 1965, the Master Aetherius announced the end of Phase One of Dr. King's mission on earth and the start of Phase Two. The following announcement was delivered through Dr. King while he was in a specialized yogic trance condition used for receiving such transmissions:

"Good afternoon.

"At this time, I have an important announcement to make to all those who wish to avail themselves of a great and mighty opportunity. It is fitting that I should now make an official announcement to the effect that, Phase One of the mission to Terra [Earth] given to primary terrestrial mental channel, or the man you call George King, is over. This Phase has been a very difficult and arduous one. Many setbacks have been overcome

"In the next Phase, all Members of The Aetherius Society will be asked to share the responsibility. You have never done this yet. Although more than once you were asked to do so, few ever responded. In the next Phase you will be expected to respond. Some time ago, I told you to watch by day and night lest your opportunity passed you by. Now I will make a statement and give to you your next opportunity.

"The Aetherius Society is now being given a new mission. This new mission will be to erect a temple of certain proportions, so that it may act as a power stabilizing station for certain spiritual energies. When this temple has been erected, then further directives will be delivered regarding its outer and inner functions. These will be unique and absolutely essential for the stabilization of transmitted energies prior to the great change."

The Master Aetherius, March 15th, 1965.

This was the first indication Dr. King received that he would be expected to play a part in creating a greatly expanded radionic machine with diverse duties to be housed within a shape power temple. The first step along those lines was to acquire a property to build a shape power temple. This is a temple that uses the science of shape power to enhance the energies invoked within its walls. The property for such a temple was purchased that year in Hollywood, California. In a later transmission given on August 26th, 1967, it became clear that the need for expanded radionic machines to transmit certain spiritual energies was more urgent than building the shape power temple itself. Such an advanced temple would cost millions of dollars, and require cutting edge technology in building materials, not to mention the difficulty in erecting a controversial building within an urban environment. Building the equipment to be housed inside the temple became the prime concern.

"You will, in the near future, redesign and rebuild both of your existing Spiritual Energy Radiators. More than ever before will we advocate the use of these Spiritual Energy Radiators during every coming Magnetization Period. Therefore, redesign is essential. After this has been done, you will then use these new machines for some time, until you are able financially and in other ways to think about building the apparatus which, eventually, will be housed in the shape power temple. You need not wait until the temple is built until you start building this machine. In fact, it would be far better to plan to build this as soon as you feel you can do so. You will build a special housing for this machine. Shape power will not be necessary in the early stages. Then build this superior machine so that you can tune into Satellite No. 3 very effectively, guide out this energy very effectively, as well as many more essential duties which can be performed by this apparatus."

The Master Aetherius, August 26th, 1967.

Through the months and years that these two earlier spiritual energy radiating machines were being used, the Cosmic Masters found them to be of tremendous value. They allowed more energy to be radiated to a world in desperate need. The Cosmic Masters now felt that it was time to upgrade these machines to increase the amount of energy that could be sent out during these difficult times. In the above transmission, they requested that Dr. King first increase the efficiency of these existing machines. They then requested that Dr. King take the next step and invent a more powerful radionic machine with "many more essential duties."

Dr. King was getting on with many other vital moves in addition to his radionic designs. By early 1970, the time of the next transmission on the subject of the Spiritual Energy Radiator, Dr. King had invented and performed the first phases of Operation Sunbeam. As explained earlier, this mission took energy from the holy mountains and transmitted it to the Mother Earth through specific psychic centers. One part of the equipment needed for this was capable of extracting energy from a radionic battery and sending this spiritual energy down through the ocean into a psychic center of Earth. Dr. King, through his advanced abilities, was able to receive certain help in the design of this Spiritual Energy Radiator from the Master Saint Goo-Ling, a prominent member of the Great White Brotherhood. By 1969, Dr. King added a component to this equipment that modified it to function as a radiating device for spiritual energies coming from Satellite No. 3. This Spiritual Energy Radiator was first used by Satellite No 3 in March, 1969. It proved so successful in this role that a duplicate machine was requested by Satellite No. 3 to be installed at the European Headquarters of The Aetherius Society in London, England. This became the upgraded Spiritual Energy Radiator that the Cosmic Masters had requested.

Even with these new, more powerful Spiritual Energy Radiators, the Cosmic Masters suggested that it was time for Dr. King to design the larger and more versatile Temple Spiritual Energy Radiator.

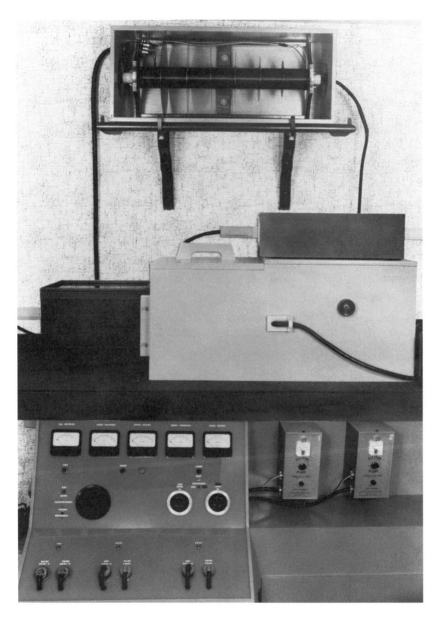

A composite photograph of the Spiritual Energy Radiator, the advanced radionic machine designed by Dr. King in the late 1960s.

"I would also like at this time to state that it is the right time in certain ways to think about inventing and building a more powerful Spiritual Energy Radiator. One which could be extremely versatile and one which could eventually be put into your shape power temple. When this is done even more energy can be collected and radiated by it and through it during future Spiritual Pushes and of course the results of this would be far reaching and of great benefit to all."

The Master Aetherius, April 14th, 1970.

The tremendous value of having The Aetherius Society operate these radionic machines in conjunction with Satellite No. 3 was very clear to the Cosmic Masters. In this transmission they are continuing the pressure for Dr. King to design bigger and better and more all-encompassing machines!

Dr. King did just this. Despite the many tasks now on his plate, he devoted considerable time to the design of the Temple Spiritual Energy Radiator. Although he had received help from the Cosmic Masters and members of the Great White Brotherhood for his earlier radionic machines, this new design was completely his own. In order to complete the magic, it was up to him to have the designs approved by the Protectors of the Flame of the Logos of Earth.

The Protectors of the Flame

These are three highly advanced intergalactic Beings who are currently living inside the planet Earth. They are here in order to help and protect the living flame or life force of the Mother Earth herself. It may seem strange that an Entity as advanced as the Mother Earth would need such help. In a way it is not so much the Mother Earth who is being helped by these great Beings – it is mankind. Dr. King has stated that if the Earth needed to protect herself from mankind, she could do so very easily, for example, by moving on her axis, thereby causing such upheaval that most of mankind would be killed through so-called natural disaster. However, with the lesson of the planet Maldek, we hypothesize that a planet may be so resistant to protecting itself against a lesser-evolved civilization that it would allow itself to be destroyed by such a race. The Protectors of the Flame are on Earth in order to protect the Mother Earth from mankind, in such a way as to allow mankind to grow and evolve as much as possible, yet being absolutely certain that mankind does not destroy the planet.

As protectors of the Mother Earth, these three intergalactic Beings have to be consulted on the implementation of any mission or radionic device that would affect the Earth herself. Operation Sunbeam clearly falls into this category. Therefore, Dr. King gained permission for this mission from these Beings prior to inaugurating it. The Temple Spiritual Energy Radiator would also fall into this category.

Partial Permission is Granted

On January 2nd, 1972, Dr. King projected into the presence of the Protectors of the Flame to present the plans for his proposed Temple Spiritual Energy Radiator. His design for this advanced radionic apparatus had three main functions:

1. Collect and transmit energies from Satellite No. 3 during a Spiritual Push out to mankind in concentrated pulses.

2. Collect and transmit energies from special prayer circles out to mankind in concentrated pulses.

3. Collect and transmit energy from the Mother Earth to the Devic Kingdom.

The first two components were fully approved by the

Lords of the Flame. However, they advised further research under field conditions on the third component, which was designed to receive and transmit energies from the Mother Earth herself. This was a very sensitive part of the machine. To release energy from the Mother Earth would not be difficult, as this takes place continuously throughout her 49 psychic centers around Earth. However, to release an exact frequency was the difficulty. Somehow Dr. King needed to draw out the exact vibration from the Mother Earth, energies that she would be releasing as a result of her Primary Initiation. How would Dr. King isolate this frequency?

It was as though this momentous meeting between Dr. King and the Protectors of the Flame sparked off a series of important events that would unknowingly answer this.

At this time, Dr. King was receiving accolades from the Cosmic Masters as well as the Protectors of the Flame for his recent invention and performance of Operation Sunbeam. Dr. King was inspired to continue his research and improvement of Operation Sunbeam. He discovered another Psychic Center of Earth located in Lake Powell, Utah, in 1972. This research project took him hundreds of hours of physically exploring and mentally tuning into the Mother Earth. Could this have been an essential part of the field research needed for Operation Earth Light as well? Though his focus at the time was on his work for Operation Sunbeam, Dr. King was discovering many hidden facets of the Mother Earth.

The following year Dr. King received a brilliant flash of inspiration that was to become the basis of the Operation Earth Light equipment. This is well described in Dr. King's book, *Visit to the Logos of Earth*.[9] His inspiration came to him in the form of a detailed image of a radionic device that he had drawn by a trained draftsman the same day. However, he was unsure at this point as to the exact function of the radionic circuit. He knew it was an antenna circuit of some type, capable of receiving and transmitting spiritual energy with a very specific wave pattern, but he was not sure how he could use it. He originally thought it might somehow be incorporated into the Operation Sunbeam equipment.

Over the next several years he often had the drawing of the new design placed in front of him and studied it for hours. He was trying to understand its exact significance. At one point Dr. King discovered during his contemplation an amazing feature of this circuit – at certain places within the physical machine itself the effects of gravity would be diminished to zero!

In 1979, during further research for Operation Sunbeam, Dr. King discovered very powerful advanced receiving and transmitting properties inherent in certain types of natural crystal. If such crystals were incorporated into specially devised radionic circuits they would form powerful devices to transmit spiritual energy over long distances. This became the basis for the next phase of Operation Sunbeam. He soon realized that this same principle could be applied to his inspired radionic circuit that he had been studying so diligently. It could function as a highly effective device to receive energies from the Mother Earth herself and transmit them out to the higher Devic Kingdom. The properties within the circuit that had come to him in a flash now started to fit exactly into place.

This was the third part of the Temple Spiritual Energy Radiator.

The different components now all fitted neatly into a whole, and the elusive Operation Earth Light equipment was very plain for Dr. King to visualize.

It was time for another visit to the Protectors of the Flame of the Logos of Earth!

On November 29th, 1979, Dr. King traveled once again in his subtle bodies for an audience with the Protectors of the

Flame of the Mother Earth. The account of this meeting is wonderfully related in *Visit to the Logos of Earth*, and I strongly urge anyone who has not yet read it to do so. For the purpose of this book I will just include the following statement from the Protectors of the Flame regarding the plans for Operation Earth Light:

> "You may proceed with this plan. You are cognizant of the fact this 'Operation Earth Light' of yours, while having our full sanction, must be regarded as a pattern only for the time being. Others will follow this pattern.
>
> "We thank you for your thought, consideration and compassion for mankind by formulating this essential plan in these troubled times.
>
> "Proceed with our Blessing."[10]

The statement, "this Operation Earth Light of yours …, must be regarded as a pattern only for the time being. Others will follow this pattern," was very prophetic indeed, as you will see in the next Chapter.

Dr. King now had the Operation Earth Light design and modus operandi fully approved. All that now remained was to put this into physical action. However, life does not always work quite that directly. Dr. King was tremendously busy with his ongoing improvements and performance of Operation Sunbeam and his continuation of Operation Prayer Power, as well as his numerous duties in running an expanding international organization, The Aetherius Society.

A Question of Balance

As stated earlier, Dr. King's design for the essential power stabilization station to be housed within the shape power temple would perform three functions.

1. Radiate spiritual energy coming from Satellite No. 3 out to the world.

2. Radiate spiritual energy invoked by prayer and mantra teams within the temple itself out to the world.

3. Receive and radiate energy from the Mother Earth to the Devic Kingdom.

By the mid-1970s the first two functions were being performed using other radionic machines.

Function number 1 was being performed every night during each Spiritual Push by the Spiritual Energy Radiators in both London and Los Angeles. These Spiritual Energy Radiators had been redesigned in 1969. Function number 2 was virtually being performed through the mission Operation Prayer Power, where energy invoked by prayer and mantra circles was being collected and sent out to the world in a concentrated form.

Operation Earth Light was now approved to accomplish function number 3; however, it had not yet been implemented. For many reasons Dr. King was unable to turn his attention to the difficult task of getting Operation Earth Light up and running. Perhaps The Aetherius Society was not destined to perform Operation Earth Light after all.

By 1981 another mission was given to Dr. King to perform, which directly related to the Devic Kingdom.

The Saturn Mission

The Cosmic Masters gave The Saturn Mission to Dr. King in September 1981. Its purpose was to promote world peace and devic stabilization. On each phase a radionic prayer battery was charged with specialized energy and then physically taken out over a psychic center of the Mother Earth. Once there, the energy within the battery was released and specially mingled with the natural energy flowing from the psychic center. Advanced Masters then carefully manipulated this energy to the Devic Kingdom and elsewhere. Could this mission have relieved the pressure for the start of Operation Earth Light? If so, it was only temporary.

Nine years later Operation Earth Light resurfaced – its time had finally arrived.

PART TWO

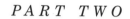

OPERATION EARTH LIGHT BEGINS

INTRODUCTION TO PART TWO

*I*n Part One I have briefly introduced the new cosmic paradigm explaining our Universe as given by the Cosmic Masters. With this foundation, Part Two reveals the details of Operation Earth Light and how it was transferred from a design of Dr. King's into a working mission being performed by the Great White Brotherhood. Observing the details of this transfer adds a valuable sense of depth to Operation Earth Light and the new cosmic paradigm.

Included in Part Two are 41 two-way communications referred to as mental transmissions between Dr. King and several advanced Masters. As we, in effect, listen in on these transmissions we hear an exciting story unfold. In addition, the transmissions can also imbue a sense of who the Masters are, how they think, and how they act. Most of us will not be ready to be in the presence of such evolved Masters for many lives, yet we can start to understand them, and therefore our own future, by letting the knowledge between the lines of these transmissions sink into our minds and souls. Remember that these are not casual conversations between ordinary people. These are communications between Dr. King and advanced Masters who have left their home worlds to spend their time helping an alien civilization that, for the most part, does not even know they exist.

I have added commentary to the mental transmissions in order to explain what was happening as observed through my eyes at the time and to add perspective. The excitement was palpable. I feel very fortunate to have been with Dr. King during this time and to have been able to record and transcribe these valuable and unique transmissions. I hope I have been able to deliver to you, the reader, a part of the intensity, excitement, and awe I felt during this important time.

I am including here a brief introduction to Dr. King's mental transmissions and the Masters who communicated in the transmissions.

Mental Transmissions

The communications presented in Part Two referred to as mental transmissions, were a form of mental telepathy. This form was much less rigorous than the kind of transmissions presented in Part One where Dr. King adopted a full yogic samadhic trance condition resulting in extremely accurate **one-way** communications. Dr. King used this earlier, and more difficult, form of trance through 1978 in order to receive from the Cosmic Masters the Cosmic Concept and other important messages for the world. Mental transmissions were used by Dr. King beginning in the late 1970s because they better suited the needs of developing his world missions such as Operation Sunbeam and The Saturn Mission. They were safe and flexible **two-way** communications with the Cosmic Masters, which could be used under field conditions as well. With Beings at the level of the Great White Brotherhood and Cosmic Masters, this form of mental telepathy is still very precise. Thoughts are composed of physical waves much as light or radio, only of a more subtle nature. The Masters are capable of receiving and sending such mental thoughts very accurately, and they also have radionic equipment to aid this transmission where necessary. Dr. King developed his expertise in this form of communication over several decades of yoga and years of communiques with these Masters.

In order for the transmission to be recorded, Dr. King verbalized his outgoing messages into a tape recorder. Then, when a response was received he repeated the response into the same tape recorder, thereby recording both parts of the communication. Though he did not go into a trance state per se, I noticed over the years of observing Dr. King during such transmissions that he often took on a portion of the personality of the Master sending the message as he relayed the information into the tape recorder. The amount of the personality or inflection of the sender depended upon such factors as who it was, the nature of the message, and the pressure of time.

Dr. King received several hundred mental transmissions in the 1980s and 1990s. He would often receive several mental transmissions in a given week. The focuses of the transmissions were quite varied, often having to do with various spiritual energy releases on behalf of mankind. Even during the period of time covered by this book, Dr. King received many more transmissions in addition to the 41 transcribed in Part Two. Dr. King was not a part time Master! He considered himself to be on duty 24 hours a day, and a transmission could often come through very late at night.

The Masters

THE MASTER AETHERIUS: This is a very advanced Cosmic Master who initially contacted Dr. King in 1954. More than any other entity, the Master Aetherius is responsible for Dr. King's mission on earth. Dr. King went to the Master Aetherius for advice and help pertaining to his mission several times over the years. However, Dr. King always preferred to stand on his own two feet as much as possible.

Though classifying the advanced Beings according to hierarchy is difficult, the Master Aetherius does have a higher "rank" than the Adepts mentioned later, and all members of the Great White Brotherhood, as he has evolved onto high-er arenas of experience.

THE LORD BABAJI: This Master has been written about throughout the ages and is the spiritual and practical leader of the Great White Brotherhood. He is more advanced than any other member of the Great White Brotherhood. He came from another more evolved planet rather than being an Ascended Master from earth, as are most of the other members of the Spiritual Hierarchy. He is here to help mankind as much as he possibly can. In fact, the Lord Babaji is so committed to helping mankind that he has been helping us as long as we have been on earth. We have been told that he plans to stay on earth until he is no longer needed by humanity.

THE ADEPTS: We have been informed of several interplan-etary Adepts who are now helping mankind. Twelve of these have been given the designation of Nixies Zero Zero One through Twelve. Three have been born into earth physical bodies. They are Nixies Zero Zero One, Nixies Zero Zero Two, and Nixies Zero Zero Three. They have taken on the limita-tion of an earth physical body in order to manipulate karma on our behalf and to enable them to carry out certain very sensitive tasks for mankind. The others are not encumbered with an earth physical body but rather inhabit a type of trav-eling body known as a third aspect body. They are able to operate on the physical plane or any of the more subtle planes around earth. Their bodies and the type of spacecraft they use can vibrate onto different planes of existence in the blink of an eye.

ADEPT NIXIES ZERO ZERO FIVE: This Being has been around earth since the mid–1960s. He has been particularly close to Dr. King in his mission to earth. They have in fact worked very closely together in many missions, The Saturn Mission being the most recent.

ADEPT NIXIES ZERO ZERO NINE: This Adept is relatively new to earth, having come to help mankind in 1988. He was originally assigned to Satellite No 3, the spacecraft that comes into orbit of earth four times a year to send out uplifting spiritual energy. Adept Nixies Zero Zero Nine, in addition to Adept Nixies Zero Zero Eight and Adept Nixies Zero Zero Seven, has been assigned to earth to aid in the transition when Adepts Nixies Zero Zero One, Nixies Zero Zero Two, and Nixies Zero Zero Three pass away from earth when their physical earth structures die.

Other Adepts also have important duties on earth during this pivotal time but they did not communicate with Dr. King regarding Operation Earth Light and so have not been included here. More can be learned about the Adepts and their missions on earth through other works listed in the bibliography.

CHAPTER 5

THE OFFER

*I*n August 1990, Dr. King again turned his attention to Operation Earth Light. The occasion was a conference of the International Directors of The Aetherius Society, and the question of the future of Operation Earth Light was brought up by the Board. Dr. King was 71 years of age and in fragile health. He realized that he would not be able to go through the rigors of fine tuning the design and overseeing the construction of the Earth Light equipment. This would entail a great deal of work and travel and he did not believe he would be able to do justice to the importance of the mission. However, he strongly felt that the mission must be performed as the Protectors of the Flame had already accepted it. There was only one organization on earth capable of picking up such an evolved and delicate operation – the Spiritual Hierarchy of Earth. With this idea in mind, Dr. King decided to consult with the Master Aetherius on this significant move.

Mental Transmission #1
Saturday, August 11th, 1990 – 9:45 a.m. PDT
American Headquarters – Los Angeles, California
With the Master Aetherius.

Dr. King: It is Saturday August 11th, Los Angeles. The time is 9:45 a.m. Pacific Daylight Time. This is a question that I will ask the Master Aetherius.

(PAUSE)

Master Aetherius, I would like to ask your advice on the following very important subject – Operation Earth Light.

As you know Operation Earth Light was accepted by the Protectors of the Flame in 1972 and later the true acceptance came in 1979.

I have made a minor start on the mission in that some equipment has been drawn up but not designed. The whole operation will need one or two years of research in order to do it justice.

Sorry about the long preamble, but this is the main question.

May I seek your advice as to whether I should, in view of certain limitations that I now face, offer the drawings of my basic equipment for Operation Earth Light to the Lord Babaji?

1. I feel that if the Great White Brotherhood were to really take up Operation Earth Light in a serious manner, they could do the mission far more justice than The Aetherius Society could.

2. Operation Earth Light could not only operate on the higher planes, but I feel that the main base should be on the physical realms of earth and, if necessary, I could give them my opinions of why this is so.

That is the end of my question at this time. Could I have your advice please?

The Master Aetherius: Very excellent idea. You should go through with it. You will have to make the initial move, as you know. However, I will give all my help and support I can to this project. You are right, the Great White Brotherhood should take it up seriously and I think they will grasp at your drawings, which you can show to them and they can use.

Those drawings have been approved by the Protectors of the Flame have they not?

Dr. King: Yes Master Aetherius, they have.

The Master Aetherius: Very well, all the more reason that the project should go ahead.

Dr. King: Yes Master Aetherius, I hope to contact the Lord Babaji in the next day or so and it will not be from this office.

Thank you for allowing me to bring this question forward in this office, as my departure to Santa Barbara has been delayed slightly.

The Master Aetherius: This is Aetherius now divorcing contact for the time being.

Dr. King: This is Dr. King now closing down communication with the Master Aetherius for the time being with a joyous heart for your helpful advice.

This communication broke the ice, as it were. On such important questions, Dr. King would often spend much time preparing the question before opening up actual transmission with the Master Aetherius. In this case, Dr. King, Richard Medway (another close aide and disciple of Dr. King), and I worked on the question for some time, going through several drafts in order to get it just the way Dr. King wanted it. This relieved some of the pressure for Dr. King during the transmission itself. Although he had many years practice in such mental transmissions it was very difficult to maintain the level of concentration necessary to hold a clear channel with the Master Aetherius, as well as think deeply and clearly about such an important subject.

The office Dr. King refers to is his office at the American Headquarters of The Aetherius Society in Los Angeles, California. Santa Barbara refers to Dr. King's private home in Santa Barbara, a seaside resort about 90 miles north of Los Angeles. Dr. King always preferred to work on such important tasks in Santa Barbara, as he was much less likely to be interrupted with day to day business there and was able to control his environment to a greater extent. His home was set up with recording facilities, as well as a word processor for transcription.

You can tell from Dr. King's last line how happy and relieved he was with the Master Aetherius's stamp of approval on his proposed transfer. Although the transfer had not been formerly approved, Dr. King knew that if the Master Aetherius agreed to it, it was going to happen!

A few days later, Dr. King left for Santa Barbara in order to take the next step of contacting the Lord Babaji directly and offering the mission to the Great White Brotherhood.

Mental Transmission #2
Wednesday, August 15th, 1990 – 10:10 a.m. PDT
Santa Barbara, California
With the Lord Babaji, Adept Nixies Zero Zero Nine, Adept Nixies Zero Zero Five, and the Master Aetherius.

Dr. King: This is Dr. King, Wednesday, August 15th, 1990, opening up communication with the Master Aetherius. The time now is approximately 10:10 a.m. PDT, Santa Barbara.

Yes Master Aetherius, thank you very much.

Master Aetherius, as requested by you in a transmission on August 11th, 1990 in Los Angeles, you gave instructions that I should contact you before opening up negotiations with the Great White Brotherhood through the Master Babaji regarding the drawings of the proposed Operation Earth Light apparatus.

I am about to open up those negotiations.

The Master Aetherius: Very well, open up the negotiations with Babaji. I have already taken the liberty of filling him in with some of the details, and he is very interested indeed. I will monitor your talk to him.

63

Dr. King: Thank you very much. I will try and contact him.

The Master Aetherius: He will be immediately available.

The Master Aetherius had notified the Lord Babaji that Dr. King wished to communicate with him, and, respecting the frail health of Dr. King as well as the importance of the communication, the Lord Babaji was standing by.

Dr. King: Thank you, Master Aetherius.

This is Dr. King opening up communication with the Master Babaji on the point that the Master Aetherius has already spoken to you about.

Yes Master Babaji, thank you very much for your very prompt reply.

I take it you are familiar with the mental communication between myself and the Master Aetherius on August 11th, 1990 from Los Angeles?

The Lord Babaji: Yes I am.

Dr. King: Do you want me to the scan that communication?

The Lord Babaji: Unnecessary.

Dr. King: What is your opinion of this move?

The Lord Babaji: We would be most delighted and honored to take over the full responsibilities of what you call Operation Earth Light. That is a good name for it and we will keep that name.

Dr. King: Thank you very much, Master Babaji.

The Lord Babaji: Further, it is not necessary for you to contact the Protectors of the Flame. I will do that and they will agree with this move – it is your invention in the first place.

The Lord Babaji was very eager to accept Operation Earth Light and he was also very sure that the Protectors of the Flame would agree with this. The importance of the statement, "it is your invention in the first place" is worth considering. The more advanced Beings always follow correct protocol, for it is an important aspect of karma. Dr. King had designed the equipment for Operation Earth Light and had a basic modus operandi worked out for its performance, which had been approved by the Protectors of the Flame in 1979. The next move had to be Dr. King's. Offering the mission to the Great White Brotherhood was not changing its modus operandi, but was actually ensuring that it would indeed be performed.

Dr. King: Thank you very much, Master Babaji.

The one thing I do have to offer you is the drawings, which have been approved by the Protectors of the Flame, by the way. We have not as yet done a great amount of research on Operation Earth Light.

The Lord Babaji: I understand that.

Dr. King: Yes, would it be possible for you to scan these drawings so you can understand them, or should I ask Adept Nixies Zero Zero Nine, who I understand is working closely with you, to scan them and then you can have what details we have available. They must have some excellent scanning equipment there. They can project a three dimensional image for you and also store it in their computer system for further reference.

They are now getting down to the practical details of the transfer here. The drawings Dr. King had were exceptionally valuable, as they had been approved by the Protectors of the Flame themselves. The mode of transfer was to place the drawings outside in the backyard of Dr. King's home in Santa Barbara. Then, Adept Nixies Zero Zero Nine would bring in a small craft and hover above the house. This craft would be rendered invisible using a type of cloaking device capable of rotating light around the craft. Once in place, the craft would then make a scan of the drawings with some type of advanced scanning machine, capable of rendering the two dimensional drawing into a three dimensional image, possibly similar to a hologram.

The Lord Babaji: That would be very nice indeed. This seems as though it is one more thing I owe to you.

A very advanced Master, the Lord Babaji displays the refined manners of a gentleman here and freely admits to Dr. King how much he owes to him for offering Operation Earth Light to the Great White Brotherhood.

Dr. King: No, that is not true, I do not take it as any debt or anything like that. It is just something which I cannot do justice to at the present time, and I am sure you can.

Dr. King, displaying the same gentlemanly quality, politely refuses to acknowledge the debt.

The Lord Babaji: We will do justice to it.

God Bless you, my son, and thank you.

Here, the Lord Babaji gives away a clue to his true spiritual height. When I heard the actual transmission of this statement, there was such a loving and high spiritual quality to the tone that it brought tears to my eyes. And this was from a mental transmission without any trance condition involved!

Dr. King: Shall I arrange the scan right away?

The Lord Babaji: Please do so, Nixies Zero Zero Nine does know where I am.

Dr. King: Thank you very much. I will arrange that scan for you.

This is Dr. King to Adept Nixies Zero Zero Nine.

(Nixies Zero Zero Nine responds but is not put on the recorder.)

Yes Nixies Zero Zero Nine, are you familiar with the short conversation between myself, the Master Aetherius, and the Lord Babaji this morning?

Adept Nixies Zero Zero Nine: Yes, and I am able to scan the drawing. I suggest that it be put outside for me on a flat table – not like the way it is now.

At this point the drawing was inside the house on a table being held down with various paperweights.

Dr. King: Yes, we will do that for you. Are you ready now?

Adept Nixies Zero Zero Nine: I am.

Dr. King: We will make sure there are no obstructions overhead, except telephone wires and the like.

Adept Nixies Zero Zero Nine: I will not need to come that near.

Here we are privileged to listen in on a seemingly straightforward scanning of the drawing by Adept Nixies Zero Zero Nine. Although Dr. King is in a physical structure and has not been using cosmotronic scanning devices, he is very aware of the potential problems Adept Nixies Zero Zero Nine may encounter. Cosmotronic is a term used to describe the advanced science of manipulating subtle energies as practiced by the Cosmic Masters.

Dr. King: Thank you, Nixies Zero Zero Nine. I will arrange that now and tell you when the drawing is in position.

(PAUSE)

We placed the drawing outside in the backyard of the house on a flat table. We had actually taped the drawing down onto a piece of matte board so it was flat and unmoved by the ever-present wind. We also tried to keep the drawing away from power lines and phone lines and a comfortable distance from the house itself.

Yes, Dr. King to Nixies Zero Zero Nine. Is that in a favorable position, or do you wish it to be moved anywhere else?

Adept Nixies Zero Zero Nine: Very favorable.

Dr. King: Very well, you may start the scan and let me know when you are finished. By the way, there are some overhead wires fairly near. Very well, you will make the scan. It is actually this side up.

Any questions you may have about the image when projected, you can ask me from the office, is this right?

Thank you. This is Dr. King moving off the scene for the time being.

There was a short pause here while Dr. King moved indoors away from the area.

Yes, Nixies Zero Zero Nine. Very well I will move it.

(PAUSE)

Yes, thank you, Nixies Zero Zero Five.

Here we find that indeed Nixies Zero Zero Nine has run into problems. He asked Dr. King to have the drawings moved, which we did, but all was still not right. We do not find out exactly what the problems are and would probably not understand them anyway, as the technology of this type of scanning is way above our current level of science. However, we find that the problem seemed to be such that Adept Nixies Zero Zero Five was called in to help. He had many more years of experience in working with the type of small craft used around earth, and dealing with the limitation of having to remain in a cloaked state of invisibility.

Adept Nixies Zero Zero Five: I must say that Nixies Zero Zero Nine is doing exceptionally well, and one of them here, Nixies Zero Zero Eight, is what you may call a cosmotronic wizard.

Adept Nixies Zero Zero Five, though obviously being called in to help solve the problems encountered, takes the opportunity to applaud the efforts of Adept Nixies Zero Zero Nine and his team – again displaying the very gentlemanly qualities of the advanced Beings.

Dr. King: Well, that is very good. It is not a very easy job, but the Lord Babaji has requested that you scan it.

Thank you – Dr. King on the side.

(PAUSE)

Here there was a pause of many minutes while the scan was taking place. All of us were requested to remain inside away from the scanning radiation.

Yes, Nixies Zero Zero Five?

Adept Nixies Zero Zero Five: I have taken what I consider to be a perfect picture, and it is better than a laser print.

Though it was obvious that the cosmotronic scan would be better than a laser print, Adept Nixies Zero Zero Five often went out of his way to keep such mental transmissions light and friendly. This helped to keep Dr. King relaxed during the strain of such transmissions. This is one reason that Dr. King always felt confident dealing with Nixies Zero Zero Five.

Dr. King: I bet it is.

Adept Nixies Zero Zero Five: Leave it there for a few minutes. We will completely demagnetize the area, although these beams have little or no superfluous magnetism.

Dr. King: Thank you very much Nixies Zero Zero Five – Dr. King on the side.

Adept Nixies Zero Zero Five: Operation "picture taking" is now finished.

Dr. King: Very well, the time now is 10:35 a.m. PDT.

Yes gentlemen – this is Dr. King. I will approach the picture if I may. I think I will close the recorder down as this is classified information.

Dr. King then proceeded to relay some classified information to the Adepts pertaining to the drawing. They would have added Dr. King's comments to their "computer file" containing the scanned design.

I have explained the drawing to Nixies Zero Zero Five and Nixies Zero Zero Nine, and they seem to be satisfied with the explanation and they will now show it to the Master Babaji. I have also answered questions about it which are strictly classified and are not on the recorder.

This is Dr. King divorcing communication with Nixies Zero Zero Nine and Nixies Zero Zero Five at the present time and standing by. Dr. King out.

(PAUSE)

Following the explanation of the drawing by Dr. King, Adept Nixies Zero Zero Five wanted to go back and take a more detailed scan of the antenna section of the drawing. There was a pause while this was taking place.

The Master Aetherius had been monitoring the whole operation and now said something to Dr. King that was not recorded; probably something similar to "how did it go?"

Yes Master Aetherius, yes it looks as though it went very well indeed. They are now studying the picture. I have given a brief rundown on my ideas. It is very simple and yet something which has to be built correctly.

Yes, the Master Babaji was very happy to have it and confirmed that the Great White Brotherhood will conduct Operation Earth Light.

I am waiting for them to ask one more question – my opinion as to why the main base, you can have several machines, but why the main one should be on the physical ground or under the physical ground, whichever way they want to go with it.

The Master Aetherius: I have scanned it – rather ingenious, what?

Another illustration of the status of the Master Aetherius;

71

somehow he independently arranged for a scan of the design and had analyzed it while the Adepts were working on the second scan. He exclaimed to Dr. King how ingenious the design was.

Dr. King: Thank you. It is something that came to me like a flash out of the blue. We would have worked on it, but the Great White Brotherhood will do the whole project far more justice than The Aetherius Society can at the moment.

Thank you very much indeed, Master Aetherius. This is Dr. King now standing by for any further questions which may be necessary.

The Master Aetherius: Aetherius out.

Dr. King: Yes, Nixies Zero Zero Five.

Adept Nixies Zero Zero Five: I have finished taking the second picture and the area has been demagnetized, not that there is any magnetism present but just in case.

Dr. King: Thank you very much. The time is now 11:00 a.m. I can take that picture away now?

Thank you. This is Dr. King proceeding to do that.

To anyone concerned I am going to have a tape scan to make sure we have covered all the points.

(The tape was played back.)

I have just played the tape back – I think all points are covered.

Yes, Nixies Zero Zero Five – don't tell me you wandered through all that tape?

Adept Nixies Zero Zero Five: I did.

Once the second scan had been taken and the plans brought back inside, Dr. King proceeded to play back the tape recorded communication he had been keeping of the transmissions up to that point. Dr. King often did this, in order to make sure he had included all the points, and more importantly, that he had translated them correctly from the telepathic thoughts sent to him into the spoken English as recorded onto the tape recorder. Both Adepts Nixies Zero Zero Five and Nixies Zero Zero Nine listened through the fairly long tape. Dr. King was always very apologetic when he did this, because he realized how slow this form of communication was in relation to the fast transfer of thoughts practiced by the more advanced Beings.

Dr. King: The one point that I was going to bring up and explain was my idea that the main base should be on the physical ground or underneath it – in more ways than one.

Adept Nixies Zero Zero Five: That is not necessary. That is well appreciated, and they know about that.

I do agree, together with Nixies Zero Zero Nine, that the report on the tape recording that you have is true and accurate even though the classified information is left out.

Here both Adepts Nixies Zero Zero Five and Nixies Zero Zero Nine agree with the contents of the tape.

Dr. King: Thank you very much indeed, Nixies Zero Zero Five and Nixies Zero Zero Nine and all concerned with this operation.

The time now is 11:25 a.m.

This is Dr. King now out.

Adept Nixies Zero Zero Five: Nixies Zero Zero Five now out.

CHAPTER 6

AETHERIUS THINKS

The Masters, due to their advanced state of evolution, can see and feel the workings of God through karma much more than mankind can. In Operation Earth Light they could see and feel the tremendous potential to help the Mother Earth and humanity at this critical time. This was not a vague belief or theory, but knowledge born out of centuries of living and working within the Laws of God. They knew that the time for Operation Earth Light had come. The pressure of karma was manifesting. The Masters knew it was time to act – and they did!

Within just a few hours of Dr. King transferring the drawing to the Lord Babaji, the mission started to take physical form.

In the next report and several that follow, Dr. King received information in the form of an information flash. This was a one-way mental transmission or flash that was not recorded during the transmission itself. This type of communication was used when the report was very short and there was no need for Dr. King to respond. In the following cases Dr. King put the information down on tape in his own words within a short time of receiving it.

Transmission #3
Wednesday, August 15th, 1990 – 5:35 p.m. PDT
Santa Barbara, California
With: Unknown, probably Adept Nixies Zero Zero Five.

Dr. King: This is Wednesday, August 15th, 1990, Santa Barbara. The time now is 5:35 p.m. PDT.

I have just received some information. The Master Babaji has already visited the Protectors of the Flame. According to my report, from an impeccable source, they have fully agreed that the Great White Brotherhood should take over the mission Operation Earth Light. The Master Babaji is already calling together some highly trusted technicians to help build this apparatus, which apparently he is very impressed with.

There will be more information coming through at a later time about the amazing happenings which are now taking place in Operation Earth Light – even though the negotiations finished but a few hours ago.

One can see the great importance placed upon Operation Earth Light by the Lord Babaji. Within just a short time he had already visited and gained the permission from the Protectors of the Flame for the Great White Brotherhood to assume responsibility for the mission. The technicians referred to here are highly evolved members of the Great White Brotherhood with a developed expertise in radionic design and construction.

The next news update staggered Dr. King and all who first heard it. It illustrated beyond a shadow of a doubt the importance the Master Aetherius placed upon Operation Earth Light.

Transmission #4
Wednesday, August 15th, 1990 – 5:40 p.m. PDT
Santa Barbara, California
With: Unknown, probably Adept Nixies Zero Zero Five

Dr. King: The time now is 5:40 p.m. I have received further information, which is to be put into my own words.

When the Master Aetherius scanned the apparatus this morning he was so impressed that, in his words:

I collected together a few of my spare parts, built them all up into one and thought into being a working model of the apparatus - which because of its very nature, will only last the maximum of seven to fourteen days. However, this will give the Great White Brotherhood something to go on as a working model.

The Master Aetherius is a very advanced Master from a civilization millions of years beyond our own. He has reached the stage of evolution where he is capable of forming several "bodies" and can control each of them with his expansive mind. As stated in *The Nine Freedoms*,[11] some of the Masters from Saturn can inhabit up to 1,860 bodies at the same time. Here, the Master Aetherius states that he brought together some of these bodies and built them up into one, so that he would have a greater concentration of his power. With this added power, he was able to "think together" a working model of the apparatus designed by Dr. King. This was a physical machine composed of physical metals and crystals created just with his mind! He was able to control the pranas from the Sun so as virtually to create matter. In this case what was created was a very large and intricate radionic machine capable of working in conjunction with the Logos of the Planet Earth. This is way above the type of manifestations per-

Here Dr. King is shown taping a mental transmission at his home in Santa Barbara, California.

formed by earth Masters more commonly known on earth. The time limit on this structure was not due to it being in any way unstable. Rather, it was due to a karmic limit on how long such direct help could be received by mankind from so evolved a Being.

I have further information about this so-called working model; however, it is classified at this time.

That is what the Master Aetherius has done since just after 11:00 a.m. this morning!

Transmission #5
Wednesday, August 15th, 1990 – Between 5:45 p.m.
and 6:00 p.m. PDT
Santa Barbara, California
With the Master Aetherius

Dr. King: I am not prepared to take a transmission, however let's go. Master Aetherius, yes.

Dr. King was not in a convenient position to receive this transmission, however did so anyway.

The Master Aetherius: It is absolutely correct what I have done, with your permission of course. This will speed things up quite a lot.

Dr. King: Yes, I have received the classified information, absolutely fantastic. I will put it off. (The tape recorder was put off for a short time) Yes, Master Aetherius?

The Master Aetherius: That is what I rather thought, and we will go ahead with that. Aetherius out.

Dr. King: Dr. King now out.

In this transmission classified information was exchanged between the Master Aetherius and Dr. King. This was not placed on the tape recorder due to its classified nature. It related to the type and purity of metal used in the model and other working details. As always, when one goes from a two-dimensional drawing on paper to a three dimensional working prototype, many questions arise. The Master Aetherius could have easily decided for himself what would be the best way to create such a prototype; however, this would not have been following the correct protocol. It was Dr. King's design in the first place, and it was proper to consult him regarding any questions or proposed modifications.

Secondly, as Dr. King was in an earth physical body, a design coming from his mind carries a much stronger karmic manipulation for mankind than a design from someone of the advancement as the Master Aetherius.

Transmission #6
Thursday, August 16th, 1990 – 1:00 p.m. PDT
Santa Barbara, California
With Adept Nixies Zero Zero Nine

Dr. King: Further progress report on Operation Earth Light. It is really amazing. According to Adept Nixies Zero Zero Nine, the model is in a Great White Brotherhood retreat, which shall not be mentioned. It has a cosmotronic link to a module, which has been given to the Lords of the Flame. They have deposited it in a certain position.

The mission has now really taken off. Not only is the Master Aetherius involved, but so too are the Protectors of the Flame. They have activated the cosmotronic link between the antenna designed by Dr. King and a collection device placed in a key location of the body of the Mother Earth by the Protectors themselves. You will recall from earlier that Dr. King discovered the principles of this type of link in his research into Operation Sunbeam back in 1978 and it became the final breakthrough in the design of Operation Earth Light. Of course, to Masters of the caliber of the Protectors of the Flame, knowledge of this type of link is as basic as the ABCs of our language.

The whole apparatus is now working. The Master Aetherius has become as involved as he possibly can in this.

This is only a small model – the main machine is only a few feet tall. However, it is up and working, which is helping the technicians of the Great White Brotherhood determine how they will adjust the permanent apparatus, which they will soon be constructing.

This report came through today, August 16th, 1990, just before 1:00 p.m. Santa Barbara. I will bring you more news when I can give it to you.

Approximately 26 hours after the Master Aetherius scanned this drawing, the model he thought together is now working.

This is your cosmic reporter standing by for further reports.

Dr. King loved to inject humor and a sense of fun into very serious and important matters. Here he is calling himself "your cosmic reporter" due to the speed and number of the reports he found himself taking on this fast-breaking story.

Transmission #7
Thursday, August 16th, 1990 – 1:10 p.m. PDT
Santa Barbara, California
With Adept Nixies Zero Zero Five

Dr. King: This is Thursday, August 16th, The time now is 1:10 p.m. I have just had further information come through – this time from Nixies Zero Zero Five, who told me that the Protectors of the Flame have sent their best wishes and congratulations to me. They will make this more official at a later date.

That is all for now.

Here a statement comes through and is almost glossed over by Dr. King. However, it is a very important statement coming from the most evolved Beings on the planet Earth – the Protectors of the Flame themselves.

Transmission #8
Thursday, August 16th, 1990 – 1:17 p.m. PDT
Santa Barbara, California
With Adept Nixies Zero Zero Two

Dr. King: The time now is 1:17 p.m. August 16th, – another report is coming through at the moment.

Yes, Nixies Zero Zero Two, this is Dr. King. Are you there?

Adept Nixies Zero Zero Two: I am taking an avid interest in the whole matter. It is beginning to build at a lightning-like speed.

I will contact you at a more opportune time.

Dr. King: Well, thank you very much. This is Dr. King.

Adept Nixies Zero Zero Two: I send you all my blessings and mental support in this operation.

Dr. King: Thank you very much.

Adept Nixies Zero Zero Two: Until later.

Dr. King: Thank you. This is Dr. King now out.

Adept Nixies Zero Zero Two: Nixies Zero Zero Two – now divorce.

Adept Nixies Zero Zero Two is one of the Three Adepts in an earth physical body. He has worked very closely with Dr. King on many occasions, especially in the 1960s and 1970s. Direct communication in the form of mental transmissions with Adept Nixies Zero Zero Two is very rare indeed. He is considered one of the preeminent experts on computers, electronics and cosmotronics, so his interest in the Operation Earth Light apparatus is not surprising.

Transmission #9
Thursday, August 16th, 1990 – 4:45 p.m. PDT
Santa Barbara, California
With Adept Nixies Zero Zero Nine

Dr. King: This is Thursday, August 16th, 1990, Santa Barbara. The time now is 4:45 p.m. Further information is coming through from Nixies Zero Zero Nine, who tells me that the prototype is working "better than expected."

I will keep you informed with the news as I receive it. This is your cosmic reporter now out.

The time now is 4:50 p.m. I have suggested a slight modification, classified, to Nixies Zero Zero Nine. They are going to think about it and they will get back to me.

Dr. King keeps his hand in the process as well. Here he sends through Adept Nixies Zero Zero Nine a suggested modification to the Operation Earth Light apparatus.

Transmission #10
Friday, August 17th, 1990 – 12:20 p.m. PDT
Santa Barbara, California
With the Master Aetherius

Dr. King: The date is August 17th, 1990. The time now is approximately 12:20 p.m. I have just had some more information come through. The Kumara of Shamballa has sent his very best wishes through the Master Aetherius and says that he is proud to have a prominent member of his most ancient Order distinguish himself so well.

The mystical Shamballa has been talked about for centuries, always surrounded by mystery. It is actually a spacecraft in geo-synchronous* orbit of earth on one of the higher subtle realms, just above where the Gobi Desert is on the

82

physical plane. In 1956 the important spiritual position of the Kumara of Shamballa was passed to the Lord Buddha. This change is in part responsible for the increased popularity of the eastern mystical traditions and is another sign of the important times in which we live. On December 5th, 1978, Dr. King was initiated into an ancient mystical order of the Spiritual Hierarchy of Earth. This initiation was in honor of the work Dr. King had done for humanity through the mission Operation Sunbeam.[12]

That is one part of it. The second part is even more amazing, in a way. The Master Aetherius is so impressed with the small model that he thought together that he is now thinking together a larger model, some 15 or 20 feet tall, keeping as near as possible to my original design.

The momentum increases!

The design I suggested they are not very keen on. However, that is what he is doing and he says he will activate that and will let me know when assembly has been finished and when it can be activated. All in all I am afraid I have caused quite a stir on this. That is all of the news flash for the moment.

Dr. King refers to the design modification he relayed to Adept Nixies Zero Zero Nine in Transmission #9. He has received back information that they have decided not to adopt this change.

---

*Geo-synchronous orbit: Where an orbiting body always remains above a certain position of earth by exactly matching the speed of earth's rotation. Many weather and communication satellites are in such orbits.

Transmission #11
Friday, August 17th, 1990 – 5:20 p.m. PDT
Santa Barbara, California
With the Master Aetherius

Dr. King: 5:20 p.m. Santa Barbara. Another report has come through from the Master Aetherius to put into my own words. He now has his second prototype on the air, much bigger than the first one. In fact, it is 22 feet in height. He stated that it really works and, "I would not expect any less from my 'Star Pupil.'"

Here the Master Aetherius refers to Dr. King as his "Star Pupil," a very clear intimation of how the Master Aetherius has been following Dr. King's progress through the ages.

Transmission #12
Friday, August 19th, 1990 – 1:45 p.m. PDT
Santa Barbara, California
With Adept Nixies Zero Zero Nine

Dr. King: Further news items. Time now is 1:45 p.m. Santa Barbara, Sunday, August 19th. Message came through from Nixies Zero Zero Nine – this is strictly classified. Permission has been granted from Mars Sector 6 for the Adepts available to help the Great White Brotherhood in the construction of Operation Earth Light modules.

Now things are going to fly.

Mars Sector 6 is a code name for the Cosmic Master in charge of Satellite No. 3. We have learned from other transmissions not included in this book that Mars Sector 6 is in command of a fleet of approximately 3,000 similar satellites that move around different parts of the galaxy, helping civilizations in the process of evolving. The Adepts fall under his line of command, so to speak. He has now authorized that they be allowed to help in the construction and manufacturing of the Earth Light equipment. This adds several capable scientists with skills and knowledge gained from more advanced civilizations to the team and will speed up the project dramatically.

Transmission #13
Friday, August 19th, 1990 – 2:00 p.m. PDT
Santa Barbara, California
With Unknown, probably Adept Nixies Zero Zero Five

Dr. King: Another news flash – 2:00 p.m., August 19th. Confirmation of the last news flash. This is correct providing only terrene materials are used and, at this present time, for exclusive use by the Great White Brotherhood and not the other planes as yet.

That confirmation was given by a source which you can fully believe. This is your cosmic reporter standing by, witnessing this fantastic scene which is happening in the Great White Brotherhood.

Within 15 minutes of the previous communication flash, Dr. King gets confirmation and more detail. Though not reported, there is a good chance that this came from Adept Nixies Zero Zero Five. This Adept was very close to Dr. King and always seemed to know what was happening. Here it is reported that there are a couple of provisos to the permission for the Adepts to help. First, they can only use material from earth. Second, they are only allowed to help construct the Earth Light equipment which will be used by the Great White Brotherhood. There are plans to extend Operation Earth Light to the higher subtle realms; however the Adepts will not be allowed to help on that project for karmic reasons.

CHAPTER 7

A VISIT TO BEN MACDHUI
AND MOUNT KILIMANJARO

*D*r. King's excitement could be felt by all of us living in his home in Santa Barbara. Operation Earth Light had eluded him for years, always in the back of his mind as a vital task waiting to be activated. Yet now, within a few days, not the months or years of his past missions, a working prototype had been made – and was working!

Finally, on August 19th, Dr. King could stand it no longer. Despite his frail health he was determined to project from his physical structure and have a look for himself at the working prototype – to see for the first time the Earth Light equipment he had seen in his mind during a flash of inspiration back in 1973.

Dr. King dictated the following description the morning after his projection.

"August 20th, 1990 – Santa Barbara. This is Monday, August 20th. The time now is 10:03 a.m. Santa Barbara. I am writing up just a short description of the experience I had yesterday, August 19th.

"On Wednesday, August 15th, at about 5:35 p.m. I received a report that the Master Aetherius had scanned the drawing of the Earth Light apparatus that was in my office. He was so impressed with the design that he thought into being an apparatus – and that did work. Later, on August 17th, we had the information that the

Master Aetherius had built a larger model of the apparatus by thought. This was again a prototype of limited lasting ability. This was 22 feet in height. I was so intrigued by this that I made arrangements to project from the body with the Adepts who would help me, in a conscious projection. This took place on Sunday, August 19th, from Santa Barbara.

"At 10:40 a.m. my aides left the room after preparing me for the projection. At 11:38 a.m. they returned back into the room again after I had had the experience."

Richard Medway and I were responsible for preparing Dr. King for this potentially dangerous projection. A fully conscious projection from the physical body is when the consciousness is placed completely in the subtle body, which then leaves the body. This can be very dangerous. One must partially raise the power of kundalini[13] up to a high center in order to remain fully conscious during the projection. Whenever the kundalini is raised there is always a potential danger. With Dr. King's advanced age and poor health, the danger was greatly increased. We prepared an oxygen tank by his bedside and administered some spiritual healing to build up his energy. Before we left him we hooked up an intercom device so that he could summon us from another part of the house if there was a problem. The Adepts were also helping during his projection. They took whatever measures necessary to aid his subtle body slide away from his physical body. Though Dr. King had done this type of projection many times in the past, his age and frail health necessitated these precautions.

Once Dr. King returned to his physical body, he required massage, oxygen, and spiritual healing to help him recover from the physical rigors of his projection. He was silent for some time afterwards. He needed time to readjust to his physical surroundings. He had been living in his subtle body in the presence of advanced Masters from the Great White Brotherhood. His senses were tuned to very high vibrations, yet he had to slip back into his frail and worn physical body with Richard and me in attendance – a shocking experience indeed!

"Although I was not feeling really up to any type of projection, I was absolutely determined to go and see these two working models of the Earth Light apparatus. I had designed it in the first place, but I had never had a chance to build one of them.

"Immediately I slid very gently out of my present surrounding, and without seeming to travel any distance whatsoever, I ended up in the Great White Brotherhood retreat in the north of Scotland which is beneath the mountain Ben MacDhui. Everything was prepared for me, and there it was in a very large room sitting on a pedestal. The 22-foot model, which the Master Aetherius had thought together, looked very beautiful to me, especially as it was illuminated by various colored lights which were fastened high up on the walls in this large room, which was part of the base under Ben MacDhui.

"I had been to the Great White Brotherhood base under Ben MacDhui many years ago which was reported in an earlier publication.[14] I found it to be an extremely active center of activities. Just a short distance away is the holy mountain, the Creag-An-Leth-Chain, from where you can just see the top of Ben MacDhui further down the valley which leads between this stretch of the Cairngorm Mountain Range near Aviemore in the north of Scotland.

"Back to the model. There are no moving parts on the model, but the base on which the model was resting was slowly spinning round so that all sides of it could be observed without continually moving around the room. I mentally asked if the colored lights could be made white so that I could inspect the model more carefully. This was immediately done, and it even looked better, in some ways, as the main antenna system was thought together by the Master Aetherius in pure gold. The Master Aetherius did gain my permission for this, since the original specifications had called for copper.

"It looked very beautiful, and it was working. It was actually picking up energy from the Mother Earth and sending these energies out for devic stabilization on earth. That was the original intention of Operation Earth Light when I first designed it. This particular prototype was 22 feet tall from the base to the top of the highest part of the antenna through which the energies were slowly pouring out. What is more, the output could be controlled by various means.

"I must say I was extremely impressed with this and highly delighted to see that Operation Earth Light, after being approved by the Protectors of the Flame in 1979, was now gradually becoming a reality.

"This prototype has a limited life of between 7 and 14 days, I am told, because after that it will have to be removed and dissolved, as it does not really belong to earth or the Great White Brotherhood or myself. The Master Aetherius made these models in order to give us all an opportunity of studying them very well and adjusting, if necessary, some of their parts so that the design could be made to be as effective as possible.

"For the record, this drawing was made from an inspiration I had on July 28th, 1973. This design was later taken in my mind to the Protectors of the Flame, who, after reading my mind, completely agreed in 1979 that Operation Earth Light should go ahead.

"Now at last, there it was in front of me slowly rotating on

a base, which was run by either a clockwork or slow elec-
tronic motor. This rotation is not necessary but very use-
ful for studying purposes. I was not the only one there
studying this. Adept Nixies Zero Zero Two was there,
Nixies Zero Zero Four, Nixies Zero Zero Seven, Nixies
Zero Zero Eight, Nixies Zero Zero Nine, the Lord
Maitreya and several picked scientists from the Great
White Brotherhood were all there making the very best
use of their time."

The Lord Maitreya is a high ranking member on the
Inner Council of the Great White Brotherhood. He has been
known of for many centuries by advanced metaphysicians
and neophytes on many different paths on earth. Several of
the Adepts were also present, as they were actively working
on the design and construction of the permanent equipment.

"When I asked if it was possible at all for me to see the
first, smaller prototype that the Master Aetherius had
built, I was told yes. In no time at all I was in the large
Great White Brotherhood retreat beneath Mount
Kilimanjaro in Africa. There it was, again displayed in a
wonderful fashion in a gigantic room. There were quite a
few people there as well, making notes. Up to the
moment, the Lord Babaji has been very careful whom he
has chosen from the Great White Brotherhood to even
view the drawings, never mind the working models themselves. They have been picked with the greatest care, and
that is the way he intends to keep it in the future. This
will not be open, even for Great White Brotherhood members, to look at. It will be turned on and off by a picked
team only, rather as we in The Aetherius Society have our
Tactical Team, as it were."

Here we learn a very interesting facet of the Great White

Brotherhood. Even within such an evolved organization of Ascended Masters, one has to earn the right to take part in the more advanced aspects of work being performed by this body. In fact just to be allowed to view the equipment is a very high honor. Dr. King compared this to the Tactical Team of The Aetherius Society, which is responsible for the performance of the sacred missions of The Aetherius Society, such as Operation Sunbeam and The Saturn Mission and the radionic equipment used.[15]

> "This model too, was working, even though it was a small model of, I would guess, about 6 or 7 feet from base to the top of the antenna. It seemed to be working very well and I had had an earlier report that even this one was working better than expected. This one also had a crystal lock on it, and the main coils were fully activated with a very low voltage of electricity.

> "Both of these machines had a cosmotronic crystal link, which cannot be used in the upcoming machines, by the way, as they have been loaned by the Master Aetherius. They are, believe it or not, locked in directly to the domicile of the Protectors of the Flame, somewhere near the center of Earth and in a secret position. In fact, so well did the large apparatus work, that they had to de-tune the cosmotronic link at one time, because the output was too great."

Here it is revealed that the two prototypes were linked to the area where the Protectors of the Flame reside. So well did the prototype and link work, they had to slightly de-tune the link at one time. This particular link will not be used in the permanent equipment. These will instead be linked to different psychic centers of the Mother Earth.

"Looking at Mount Kilimanjaro from the outside you see a huge mountain perpetually capped with snow and ice fields but inside that retreat, I must say, is very warm, very inviting, and very nicely done. The Great White Brotherhood has spent an awful lot of time and effort in preparing this retreat.

"Back in the retreat in Scotland again, I remembered vividly the last trip I had taken to the retreat beneath Ben MacDhui, and the wonderful things that happened there.

"Even as I talk, rapid strides are being made with actual manufacturing of appliances for Operation Earth Light, which has taken on a fantastic importance.

"On Saturday evening I was informed by Nixies Zero Zero Nine that Mars Sector 6 had sent forth his karmic permission for the Adepts to work in strict conjunction with the Great White Brotherhood and physically help them to build these appliances, providing they are built and placed in strategic Great White Brotherhood centers throughout the world – probably in classified positions.

"Before leaving the retreat beneath the cold bare rock of Ben MacDhui, I took one last look at this beautiful appliance, still rotating very slowly on its motor-driven pedestal, with the lights now turned from bright white to very delicate colors, mostly magenta.

"I realized that there was the manifestation of another spiritual dream come true. This greatly affected me since I myself invented the design for the apparatus in the first place and designed the mission Operation Earth Light, which will continue into the future.

"Reluctantly, I had to leave the retreat and arrived back in Santa Barbara at 11:38 a.m. on Sunday, August 19th, 1990."

CHAPTER 8

HELP FROM THE ADEPTS

With the great advantage of studying the two prototypes of the Master Aetherius, the enlightened technicians of the Great White Brotherhood, with valuable help from the Adepts, began their construction project in earnest. With the focused mental rays of such finely attuned Masters working in concert towards a karmic goal, the momentum built swiftly.

Transmission #14
Monday, August 20th, 1990 – 11:50 a.m. PDT
Santa Barbara, California
With Adept Nixies Zero Zero Four

Dr. King: This is Monday, August 20th, Santa Barbara. The time now is 11:50 a.m. PDT. This is Dr. King to Nixies Zero Zero Nine. Come in, if possible, please.

Yes, Nixies Zero Zero Four.

Adept Nixies Zero Zero Four: You cannot easily contact Nixies Zero Zero Nine.

Dr. King: No, do not disturb him, it is not in any way urgent. When he can contact me would you ask him to do that please?

Thank You. This is Dr. King out.

Adept Nixies Zero Zero Four: Nixies Zero Zero Four out.

Adept Nixies Zero Zero Nine is so immersed in the construction that he is uncontactable. In this case, Adept Nixies Zero Zero Four handles the communication on his behalf. It may seem normal for an Adept to be unavailable and have another Adept cover incoming communications. However, having been with Dr. King during hundreds of mental transmissions for over 10 years, this was very unusual. I can only think of one other instance that one of the Adepts was unavailable to answer a request for a mental transmission. At times it could take up to 10 or 15 minutes for a response, but to be uncontactable was very rare indeed and illustrates the importance placed on the Earth Light construction project by all concerned.

Transmission #15
Monday, August 20th, 1990 – 12:45 p.m. PDT
Santa Barbara, California
With Adept Nixies Zero Zero Three

Dr. King: Time now is 12:45 p.m. I have had a flash through from Adept Nixies Zero Zero Three, who is also probing about up there. In my own words: He wished to compliment me and also wished to state that there are some scientists from the Great White Brotherhood who thought they could improve upon the original design. They were huddled together for several days and the Master Aetherius gently reminded them that, "the shortest distance between two points is a straight line." And my appliance adheres to this axiom. So with glee in their hearts they packed it up, because their design had already become so complicated that the thing would take several months to build anyway – even if it worked. So they have packed it up and joined the rest of the team with what Nixies Zero Zero Three calls "a sigh of relief."

The scientists referred to were in no way trying to steal

94

the show; they are Ascended Masters who have evolved beyond such feelings. They honestly believed there was a chance that they could improve upon the design forwarded by Dr. King and felt that it was their spiritual duty to try. They had probably been studying and working on radionic devices for thousands of years. However, after a few days work and the dawning realization that they could not improve the original design, the Master Aetherius stepped in to gently remind them that simplicity is best. It is little wonder that Dr. King referred to his design as "a flash of inspiration from God."[16]

This information transmission came from Adept Nixies Zero Zero Three. He is one of the Three Adepts in an earth physical body and very well known in Aetherius Society literature. He had worked closely with Dr. King for many years, yet such a mental communication was quite rare.

I think that it is the latest from the Great White Brotherhood at the moment, except that everybody is very busy. I have really caused a stir up there, I might tell you. Although they realized the urgency of the mission right away, they have even more impetus to get their own appliances operational since the declaration from Mars Sector 6 (see Transmission #12). Apparently they are not too far away from putting their own small appliance on the air. I will let you know later on what happens.

Transmission #16
Monday, August 20th, 1990 – 12:55 p.m. PDT
Santa Barbara, California
With Adept Nixies Zero Zero Nine

Nixies Zero Zero Nine is now getting back to Dr. King following his earlier mental call.

Dr. King: Yes, Nixies Zero Zero Nine, the time now is 12:55 p.m. PDT. No, it was not urgent at all. We do not want to disturb you in any way because I understand you are quite busy there.

Adept Nixies Zero Zero Nine: I am very busy indeed, and things are running along very well. What was the question?

Dr. King then asked if Adept Nixies Zero Zero Nine could be available later that night for a short communication on a non-related classified mission.

Adept Nixies Zero Zero Nine: I think not because we are hoping to get the first module for the Great White Brotherhood on the air later on today.

Dr. King: Thank you very much. That is very good. This is Dr. King now out.

Adept Nixies Zero Zero Nine: Nixies Zero Zero Nine out.

Dr. King is requesting the time and help of Adept Nixies Zero Zero Nine on a non-related mission later that night. All the Adepts were fully aware of the difficulties under which Dr. King was operating. Here was a very special Master in an earth physical body extending the Cosmic Concept to a very backward world, as well as performing vital world operations with a tight budget using limited personnel. Because of this, the Cosmic Masters and the Adepts always went out of their way to help and be available to Dr. King when requested. One good example was how easily Dr. King was able to contact the Master Aetherius during Transmission #1 – this, a Master who does not stay on or even near Earth, as his home planet is Venus, over 25,000,000 miles away. Today, however, Adept Nixies Zero Zero Nine has a pressing deadline for the construction of the first unit of Operation Earth Light equipment and must decline Dr. King's request.

Transmission #17
Monday, August 20th, 1990 – 5:05 p.m. PDT
Santa Barbara, California
With Adept Nixies Zero Zero Nine

Dr. King: The time now is 5:05 p.m. PDT. I have a news flash coming through from Nixies Zero Zero Nine.

He says they have made the first Great White Brotherhood appliance. It is all complete except for the interlock which will be completed tomorrow.

This portion of the appliance was completed at 5:00 p.m. today. It was built to my specification, and was built by the Great White Brotherhood with the help of Adepts Nixies Zero Zero Seven, Nixies Zero Zero Eight, and Nixies Zero Zero Nine. It is expected to be fully operational on August 21st.

Following this one-way flash of information, Dr. King opens up two-way communication with Adept Nixies Zero Zero Nine.

Dr. King: Well, that is great news. How big is it from base to antenna?

Adept Nixies Zero Zero Nine: This is only a small one, and it is exactly 11 feet.

Dr. King: Oh well, that is big enough. Is the protective covering in place?

Adept Nixies Zero Zero Nine: Ready for the one last stage.

Dr. King: Thank you, Nixies Zero Zero Nine. This is your cosmic reporter going off the air. The time now is 5:06.

The first unit is complete except for the interlock or crystal link. The speed at which this equipment was constructed is amazing. It is important to remember that this is physical equipment. The actual materials, such as gold or copper or silicon or crystal, must all be acquired from the earth somewhere. This material has to be physically tooled, polished and fastened together. The members of the Great White Brotherhood and the Adepts have to physically do this. They cannot visualize it into existence like the Master Aetherius did. The physical construction standards for radionic equipment are extremely high, as Aetherius Society technicians found during the construction of radionic equipment used in other missions. In addition, the mental vibrations put into the equipment at the time of construction must be taken into account. All who worked on this equipment would have had to control their thoughts to a high degree during the construction process to keep the equipment as psychically clean and uplifted as possible. This need for mental control adds greatly to the degree of difficulty.

In just four days after the Master Aetherius thought into being the first prototype, the scientists from the Great White Brotherhood and the Adepts built the main antenna unit of the Operation Earth Light device – truly an amazing feat!

Transmission #18
Monday, August 20th, 1990 - 5:20 p.m. PDT
Santa Barbara, California
With Adept Nixies Zero Zero Nine

Dr. King: This is Dr. King to Nixies Zero Zero Nine. Thank you for your very prompt reply. I will ask the question mentally.

(PAUSE)

Yes, Nixies Zero Zero Nine, you say that, since your Master, Mars Sector 6, sanctioned your help that you are able to help with all the equipment at your disposal.

By now it must look like a work of art.

Adept Nixies Zero Zero Nine: Yes, it does. It certainly is. That is all the cosmic news for the time being. We will get back with you when we have more to report.

You can imagine the thought process of Dr. King here. He knew a little of the equipment available to the Great White Brotherhood through past associations and he knew the difficulty of radionic construction. As he thought about the feat that was reported to him in Transmission #17, he could not quite see how the appliance could have been made so quickly without some other type of help. He asked the question mentally to Nixies Zero Zero Nine so as not to give away any classified information. His thoughts were correct. It turned out that Mars Sector 6 had given his permission for the Adepts not only to help, but to use their advanced "tools" from other worlds in the construction project as well!

It may seem strange, but despite the level of advancement of the members of the Great White Brotherhood they are restricted to the type of equipment they can use while on earth. Although they are essentially on the same level of evolution as the Adepts who are from more advanced planets, they cannot use the equipment developed on these planets. They have to construct their own tools and devices themselves from earth material. This is all part of the karmic manipulation being performed by them for us. The scientists from the Great White Brotherhood could have constructed the Earth Light equipment with their own tools. However, it would have taken much longer.

This is one of the important lessons to take away from our glimpse behind the veil. The Ascended Masters of the Great White Brotherhood have achieved the pinnacle of all the religions on earth. They have achieved self-realization, or nirvana as described by our ancient religious texts, yet their experiences continue. They do not float up to the clouds, as it were, but continue to work, learn, and grow. They have problems, challenges, and lessons. Evolution continues. They are hundreds of lives ahead of mankind, yet still have a long way to go. We should remember these holy ones in our thoughts and prayers, for they are sacrificing much to stay back on earth in order to help our civilization.

Transmission #19
Monday, August 20th, 1990 – 5:45 p.m. PDT
Santa Barbara, California
With Adept Nixies Zero Zero Nine

Dr. King: Time now is 5:45 p.m. I have just heard from Nixies Zero Zero Nine that the Supreme Council of the Great White Brotherhood have voted, if that is the word, unanimously to elect me as scientific advisor to Operation Earth Light. The appointment will be offered officially in the right way to me in a day or so.

Again Dr. King responds to the one-way information flash and opens up two-way communication with Adept Nixies Zero Zero Nine.

Well I, of course, will agree, yes. It will be offered by whom?

Adept Nixies Zero Zero Nine: Nixies Zero Zero Six.

Dr. King: Oh, he has gone to his command mode has he?

Adept Nixies Zero Zero Nine: Yes he has.

Dr. King: Well, that is all the news at this hour. This is your cosmic reporter now out.

The offer to Dr. King of being appointed as scientific advisor to Operation Earth Light was more than a polite gesture. First of all, Dr. King originally developed the design of the equipment and the modus operandi. Second, the stronger the tie between Operation Earth Light and mankind, the better it is in a karmic sense. Appointing Dr. King as active scientific advisor does just this.

We also see another example of the intensity of the push for getting Operation Earth Light on the air. The Lord Babaji has changed to his "command mode," which is illustrated by his now being referred to as Adept Nixies Zero Zero Six. In his command mode, the Lord Babaji tones down his spiritual vibration to focus on getting a specific physical task completed. I have personally witnessed this change through such transmissions, and it is quite dramatic. The Lord Babaji is an aspect of an evolved Master from Saturn, which is the most evolved world in this solar system. Even during mental transmissions with Dr. King, a part of his elevated presence comes through. Such vibrations bring forth an intense and powerful feeling of love. You feel like you are melting into the arms of God Itself. Strangely, this vibration can actually slow down such physical activity as construction. Imagine tuning into a very delicate prayer or mantra and then trying to cut a piece of wood on a large and noisy table saw. The type of focus needed is very different. Consequently, the Lord Babaji tones down his vibrations here so as not to interfere but rather help with the physical push to get the equipment made. There are undoubtedly other ramifications to such a temporary change by the Lord Babaji. However, this is one that Dr. King was well aware of.

Transmission #20
Tuesday, August 21st, 1990 – 5:00 p.m. PDT
Los Angeles, California
With Adept Nixies Zero Zero Nine

Dr. King: This is your cosmic reporter back again. The time now is 5:00 p.m. Just had a news flash from Nixies Zero Zero Nine to state that the Great White Brotherhood will be on the air in their own right tomorrow morning, Wednesday, August 22nd, 1990. Yes, Nixies Zero Zero Nine, I will turn the tape off.

I just had a flash of secret information there, which delights me no end. Just a little after midnight tonight, early tomorrow morning, they will be on the air with the first appliance built by the Great White Brotherhood in Operation Earth Light. This is your cosmic reporter signing off for the time being. We will give you a newscast as soon as it comes in. End of news flash.

Transmission #21
Tuesday, August 21st, 1990 – 5:10 p.m. PDT
Los Angeles, California
With the Master Aetherius

Dr. King: Cosmic reporter is back again. The time now is 5:10. I have just had a flash from the Master Aetherius. He cryptically said, "I knew you would like that."

Yes, Master Aetherius, we surely do. This is your cosmic reporter signing off.

Dr. King receives advance notice of the important first test phase of the first unit of Operation Earth Light, first from Adept Nixies Zero Zero Nine and then from the Master Aetherius 10 minutes later. Within hours of the apparatus being built, plans have been made to test the equipment and activate the apparatus! This entails placing a linked device into a psychic center of Earth and then tuning the receiver apparatus in one of the retreats of the Great White Brotherhood to this device. This will then pull the special vibration of energy from Earth through the psychic center and out through the radiating apparatus to the higher Devic Kingdom.

Transmission #22
Wednesday, August 22nd, 1990 – 10:20 a.m. PDT
Los Angeles, California
With Adept Nixies Zero Zero Nine

Dr. King: The time now is 10:20 a.m. PDT.

Nixies Zero Zero Nine, would you come in please.

Yes, Nixies Zero Zero Nine, I take it that Operation Earth Light is now operational from the Great White Brotherhood, is that right?

Adept Nixies Zero Zero Nine: That is absolutely correct, it was operational from 1:00 a.m. this morning.

Dr. King: Thank you very much. I am just going to make a very, very brief report about this in my magazine, cutting out all the classified information.

Adept Nixies Zero Zero Nine: We are all happy about that. Already the second appliance is near the assembly stage and that will be operational in a day or so's time.

Dr. King: Thank you. This is Dr. King closing down communication at the present time.

Transmission #23
Wednesday August, 22nd, 1990 – 1:20 p.m. PDT
Los Angeles, California
With the Lord Babaji (Adept Nixies Zero Zero Six)

Dr. King: The time now is 1:20 p.m. There is a flash coming through from Adept Nixies Zero Zero Six to be put in my own words.

The apparatus is working in a brilliant fashion. Well done, Dr. King. On behalf of the Great White Brotherhood, we are indebted to you.

Thank you very much Adept Nixies Zero Zero Six.

This is the cosmic reporter now out for the time being.

It is now official – the first test of the Operation Earth Light equipment made by the Great White Brotherhood was successful. The first constructed unit was up and working!

The Lord Babaji gives the official announcement to Dr. King, and he again takes the opportunity to thank Dr. King for the mission itself.

The journey to this point in Operation Earth Light was indeed a long and involved one. It began in 1965 and finally reached fruition in 1990 – 25 years later. The journey included many lessons in radionic design, flashes of inspiration, research over two psychic centers of Earth, visits with the Protectors of the Flame, and even the direct interest of Cosmic Masters such as the Master Aetherius and Mars Sector 6. Dr. King was extremely happy and excited by this news. He felt a deep sense of accomplishment for a mission that had taken many years and pathways to find its way to this important point.

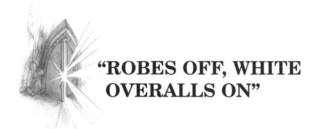

CHAPTER 9

"ROBES OFF, WHITE OVERALLS ON"

*T*he first unit of Operation Earth Light had proved to work brilliantly. However, there was much work to do before all the required equipment would be ready. This meant long hours in the construction labs of the Great White Brotherhood retreats. Operation Earth Light was to be a sensitive and complex mission, needing a wide array of finely tuned radionic equipment linked intricately with the Mother Earth.

How Operation Earth Light was Designed to Work

Operation Earth Light was designed to slowly release a part of the energy the Mother Earth received in her Primary Initiation on July 8th, 1964. This careful release would alter conditions on earth in a gradual manner, so that as many people as possible could adjust to the higher vibrations that would be present in the coming New Age.

The Equipment

There were to be seven complete units, with each unit consisting of a linked module and an antenna cluster.

The seven antenna clusters were to be built according to the design by Dr. King and would constitute the heart of each unit. Each would be housed in a different retreat of the Great White Brotherhood around earth. These retreats are within different mountains and are all on the physical level of earth.

The modules would be radionically linked to the antennae and would be placed in, or very near to, seven different psychic centers of the Mother Earth.

One module and one antenna constitute a complete circuit, which can be activated or deactivated. When activated, there exists an open path for energy to flow from the psychic center of Earth to the antenna, which then transmits this energy out to the higher Devic Kingdom.

The psychic centers of Earth are in some ways similar in function to the psychic centers of man, being subtle energy vortices transmitting and receiving energies. The Earth Light antenna is designed to make a demand on a very particular waveform or vibration of energy being held by the Mother Earth.

The Great White Brotherhood would be able to activate a single unit of Operation Earth Light, all seven units or any combination of the seven units.

Probable Additional Features

As the special energy comes through the different psychic centers of Earth there would undoubtedly be a different essence added by each psychic center. With this in mind the Great White Brotherhood would probably be able to link together the different modules with the different antennae at will in order to achieve specific results at different times.

As the antennae would be set up in different parts of the world, the Great White Brotherhood would be able to tune into the prevailing conditions of the world and activate one or more units to affect different areas at different times. This set-up would give them great flexibility, as they would be able to respond to the fluctuations of the karma of mankind as a whole as well as the karmic patterns in different areas of the world.

The Construction Continues

There was a tremendous amount of work still to be done, as each module had to be built and linked to different psychic centers of the Mother Earth. The modules, the antennae, and the different links all had to be tested, and the equipment itself had to be carefully installed. The pressure to complete this construction was still on, but the speed of construction had to slow due to the necessary testing. The excitement of the initial breakthrough had now changed to a careful, methodical construction and testing phase. Dr. King and The Aetherius Society continued with other important missions – yet all the while anxiously watching and waiting for the official start of Operation Earth Light.

Transmission #25
Wednesday, August 29th, 1990 – 5:40 p.m. PDT
Los Angeles, California
With Adept Nixies Zero Zero Nine

Dr. King: Time now is 5:40 p.m. Los Angeles. I have just had word that the second apparatus has been fully assembled and is now being checked. I have sent my best wishes to those involved and they will let me know when the check has been completed.

This is your cosmic reporter now signing off for the time being.

Transmission #26
Friday, August 31st, 1990 – 6:04 p.m. PDT
Santa Barbara, California
With Adept Nixies Zero Zero Nine

Dr. King: A further report came through stating that the second appliance has been checked and found to be workable.

The first appliance has been taken off the air. The prototypes, which were previously built by the Master Aetherius, have now been dissolved.

This is your cosmic reporter reporting from Santa Barbara on the latest information regarding Operation Earth Light on Friday, August 31st. The time now is 6:04 p.m.

Your cosmic reporter now out and standing by for further information.

The two prototypes created by the Master Aetherius were dissolved. They undoubtedly helped the construction team greatly. However, by karmic law they had to be dissolved as they did not belong to this earth. We are also told that the first appliance built by the Great White Brotherhood had been deactivated. It had been on the air for approximately nine days. This first appliance had worked well and it was now all systems go to construct the other units.

Transmission #27
Saturday, September 1st, 1990 – 12:10 p.m. PDT
Santa Barbara, California
With Adept Nixies Zero Zero Nine

Dr. King: This is your cosmic reporter again – from Santa Barbara, Saturday, September 1st, 1990. The time now is 12:10 p.m. I received another news flash that the third apparatus is now in the process of being built and assembled in Operation Earth Light.

That is all the information I have now.

Transmission #28
Sunday, September 2nd, 1990 – 12:30 p.m. PDT
Santa Barbara, California
With Adept Nixies Zero Zero Nine

Dr. King: Sunday, September 2nd, 1990 – time now is 12:30, Santa Barbara. Another news flash is coming through right now from Nixies Zero Zero Nine. I have been asked to put this in my own words.

The Spiritual Hierarchy of Earth is moving at amazing speed. They are getting along very well with the assembly of apparatus no. 3, and the materials have all been assembled together for the building of apparatus nos. 4 and 5.

It is a matter of robes off and white overalls on for the chosen team working on this project.

Thank you very much.

You must bear in mind that these Operation Earth Light units are not put together with any form of magic. They are built with terrene material. To collect this material together takes time and effort on everyone's part. They are not just thought into being but are physically made with physical materials that have to come from the planet Earth.

So it looks as though they are pushing on with tremendous skill and determination.

This is your cosmic reporter now signing off for the time being.

How different life is for members of the Great White Brotherhood than many would have imagined. These evolved Masters do not become instant Gods, so to speak, spending all their time in blissful meditation. They still act on the physical plane. They use their hands, build equipment, and operate machines. Physical equipment is still needed and used by such spiritually advanced Masters. However, such work always has a spiritual side as well. The equipment in Operation Earth Light is linked to different psychic centers of the Mother Earth. To build and position such equipment one needs an advanced sensitivity to the Mother Earth. The equipment must also be handled very carefully, as potentized spiritual energy will be flowing through it. All parts of the equipment must be kept clean both physically and psychically. All this takes a high degree of awareness, awareness gained through hundreds of lives of spiritual practice and experience in the classroom of earth.

Transmission #29
Tuesday, September 4th, 1990 – 11:20 a.m. PDT
Santa Barbara, California
With Adept Nixies Zero Zero Nine

Dr. King: This is Tuesday, September 4th, 1990. The time now is 11:20 a.m. This is Dr. King to Nixies Zero Zero Nine, please answer me when you can.

Yes, Nixies Zero Zero Nine. May I ask you a question?

Are you relating to Satellite No. 3?

Adept Nixies Zero Zero Nine: No. We are continuing with our special assignment.

Dr. King: Thank you very much. That will mean all the time, will it?

Adept Nixies Zero Zero Nine: Yes, it will.

Dr. King: Thank you. That is all I wanted to know.

Adept Nixies Zero Zero Nine: I will have a further report as soon as possible regarding apparatus no. 3.

Dr. King: You are getting along very well.

Thank you very much. This is Dr. King breaking contact.

Adept Nixies Zero Zero Nine: Nixies Zero Zero Nine now out.

Satellite No. 3 had come back into orbit of earth the previous day, September 3rd. Dr. King is asking if Adept Nixies

Zero Zero Nine, along with Nixies Zero Zero Eight and Nixies Zero Zero Seven, were going to report back to Satellite No. 3 and work on other projects or would be allowed to continue their work on the Earth Light equipment. The answer was that they would continue on the Earth Light project, which was great news for all who were working on the project.

Transmission #30
Monday, September 10th, 1990 - 10:00 a.m. PDT
Los Angeles, California
With Adept Nixies Zero Zero Nine

Dr. King: It is 10:00 a.m. Monday, September 10th, 1990 – Los Angeles. This is your cosmic reporter to Nixies Zero Zero Nine.

Yes, Nixies Zero Zero Nine, I am just closing my magazine now. One last question, have you finished apparatus no. 3 yet?

Adept Nixies Zero Zero Nine: They have just finished the assembly on apparatus no. 3 and it is now going on to the usual thorough test procedures. It will not be put in full operation for several days.

Dr. King: Thank you very much indeed. This is your cosmic reporter now signing off.

Dr. King was finishing an issue of *Cosmic Voice*, the official journal of The Aetherius Society. He always liked to keep members of The Aetherius Society and interested subscribers up to date on important events through *Cosmic Voice*. Although he kept most of the aspects of Operation Earth Light secret at that time, he wanted to release as much information as he was allowed to in the coming issue.

Transmission #31
Tuesday, September 25th, 1990 – 12:00 noon PDT
Santa Barbara, California
With Adept Nixies Zero Zero Nine

Dr. King: It is Tuesday, September 25th, 1990. This is your cosmic reporter, reporting at the present time regarding Operation Earth Light to Nixies Zero Zero Nine.

Do you have any further reports about Operation Earth Light, please?

This is Dr. King standing by.

Yes, Nixies Zero Zero Nine. It is Tuesday, September 25th, 1990, Santa Barbara. Time now is 12:00 noon.

Adept Nixies Zero Zero Nine: Yes, the whole Operation Earth Light is going very well indeed. I gave you the report on September 2nd, about apparatus nos. 4 and 5. They have now been assembled and are being rigorously tested.

Dr. King: Thank you very much indeed. That is great news. I will pass that along.

Yes, Nixies Zero Zero Nine?

Adept Nixies Zero Zero Nine: I would like to extend to you from myself and my two companions heartiest congratulations on your magnificent Operation Sunbeam. May it last long and be successful.

Dr. King: Well, thank you very much, Nixies Zero Zero Nine, I deeply appreciate that.

This is Dr. King now out.

Adept Nixies Zero Zero Nine: This is Nixies Zero Zero Nine now out.

There had been commemoration services throughout The Aetherius Society the night before to celebrate the start of

Operation Sunbeam on September 24th, 1966. Adept Nixies Zero Zero Nine wished to express his great respect for this valuable mission to its designer, Dr. King. This was one of the many missions being performed by Dr. King and The Aetherius Society while the transfer of Operation Earth Light to the Great White Brotherhood was progressing. Beings at the stage of evolution of Adept Nixies Zero Zero Nine understand very clearly how important such karmic missions are for our world.

Transmission #32
Monday, October 9th, 1990 – 5:25 p.m. PDT
Los Angeles, California
With Adept Nixies Zero Zero Nine

Dr. King: This is your cosmic reporter – position Los Angeles – time 5:25 p.m., date October 9th, 1990. Yes, Nixies Zero Zero Nine. Yes it is, it is always a sad time for us. However, you are staying?

Adept Nixies Zero Zero Nine: Yes, we are staying on the Earth Light project.

Dr. King: Very well. Will you keep me up to date with that as much as you can when you are able?

Adept Nixies Zero Zero Nine: Yes, but I wanted to make sure that you realized that we were still messing around on earth.

Dr. King: Oh, you're learning the idiom now?

Thank you very much.

This is Dr. King terminating communication for the time being with Nixies Zero Zero Nine.

Adept Nixies Zero Zero Nine: Nixies Zero Zero Nine out.

Satellite No. 3 left earth at 5:00 p.m. PDT on October 9th

(12 midnight GMT). This is a sad time, especially for Dr. King who was more aware of Satellite No. 3's presence than most on earth. As mankind becomes more sensitive to the activities of this satellite many more will feel a sense of sadness each time it leaves earth's orbit in the future.

We learn that Adept Nixies Zero Zero Nine and Team were again staying on earth to work on the Earth Light equipment. In fact, Adept Nixies Zero Zero Nine and Team have remained on earth ever since their arrival here in 1988.

"Messing around on earth"! Adept Nixies Zero Zero Nine, although engaged in very important work, is not above self-effacing humor. This was a notable characteristic in many of the advanced Masters who communicated through Dr. King. They would often use humor in their communications with Dr. King to help put him at ease. They realized the difficult job he had – paddling against the strong tide of ignorance and greed on earth.

Transmission #33
Monday, November 1st, 1990 – 11:15 a.m. PST
Los Angeles, California
With Adept Nixies Zero Zero Nine

Dr. King: This is your cosmic reporter. Time now is 11:15 a.m. Pacific Standard Time, November 1st, 1990 – Los Angeles. I have just had a report through from Nixies Zero Zero Nine regarding progress on the Earth Light apparatus.

As you know, apparatus no. 3 was built on September 10th, and materials were collected together for apparatus nos. 4 and 5. Apparatus nos. 4 and 5 have now been built and tested, and apparatus nos. 6 and 7 have been mostly assembled and are ready for a test period.

Operation Earth Light, as such, has gone on the air from time to time for testing. It has now been physically taken off the air and will be put on air at a very appropriate time in very significant positions throughout the world.

This is your cosmic reporter signing off for the present time, which is 11:20 a.m. on November 1st, 1990.

The testing procedure continued, inching nearer and nearer to the all-important commencement.

In the midst of the Operation Earth Light communications Dr. King's other responsibilities did not abate. The Aetherius Society had recently purchased a property in Arizona, very near to a psychic center of the Mother Earth in Lake Powell, Utah. The inauguration of this mission base was due to take place in early November with four phases of Operation Sunbeam. This entailed setting up the household with furniture and equipment. Dr. King was looking forward to going to this base for the upcoming phases. The house was later named Inspiration Point due to its beautiful setting along the side of Lake Powell.

Transmission #34
Monday, November 5th, 1990 – 1:00 p.m. MST
Greenehaven, Arizona (Inspiration Point)
With Adept Nixies Zero Zero Nine

Dr. King: This is your cosmic reporter. It is almost 1:00 p.m. Mountain Standard Time. Position – Inspiration Point. The date is Monday, November 5th. Yes, I have just received a report from Nixies Zero Zero Nine that apparatus no. 6 has been completed and is now undergoing rigorous tests. Apparatus no. 7 will be completed shortly.

This is your cosmic reporter signing off for the time being and on stand-by.

Dr. King recorded the famous mental transmission from the Lord Babaji on the beach at Lake Powell, Utah, a psychic center of the Mother Earth.

CHAPTER 10

PHASE ONE SUCCESSFUL!

Transmission #35
Saturday, November 10th, 1990 – 1:45 p.m. MST
Lake Powell, Utah (Near a Psychic Center of Earth)
With the Lord Babaji

Dr. King: The time now is approximately 1:45 p.m. MST. The date is November 10th, 1990. Position – the shores of Lake Powell, Utah. I am standing by for an important message to come through.

The Lord Babaji: On November 11th, 1990, three units of Operation Earth Light will be activated and remain on the air for several days. We will inform you when these are taken off the air.

The position of these units is strictly classified; however, it can be announced that these units will be put on the air on November 11th, 1990.

We wish to thank you for your Operation Earth Light. This mission will become of great importance – and become global!

We would like to take this opportunity to give our most profound thanks to all who helped Operation Earth Light to become in all ways operational – and especially thank the original designer of the apparatus.

Thank you, my son.

End of communication.

Babaji.

Finally, the long-awaited announcement was given. The Lord Babaji had resumed his true spiritual nature to make the official announcement of this historic inauguration to Dr. King. The vibrations from this evolved Master were so great and the importance of the event so monumental that Dr. King was overcome with joy.

In Dr. King's own words:

"So deep was the emotional reaction felt by myself after this mental transmission that I spent some time walking up and down the flat beach and, to be honest with you, crying like a baby!

"At long last, Operation Earth Light – the mission design plans of which I had devised in 1973 – had made a serious start!"[17]

It was very fitting that this historic announcement was given to Dr. King when he was literally on the side of one of the psychic centers of the Mother Earth.

Transmission #36
Monday, November 12th, 1990 – 12:25 p.m. MST
Greenehaven, Arizona (Inspiration Point)
With Adept Nixies Zero Zero Nine

Dr. King: This is Monday, November 12th, position Inspiration Point, Lake Powell area. The latest update on the units of Operation Earth Light is that there are now 7 units completed. Units 6 and 7 have now been through rigorous testing and they have now been declared as fully operational in all ways.

The time now is 12:25 p.m. MST. Yes, Nixies Zero Zero Nine. Yes, I have indeed recorded that one. Seven units all completed. Yes, I picked it up from Nixies Zero Zero Six – fantastic. And November 11th becomes the official birthday of the mission?

Adept Nixies Zero Zero Nine: Yes, it indeed does. We were on the air on and off before with some units, but they were for test purposes only as you no doubt know.

Dr. King: Yes, thank you very much, Nixies Zero Zero Nine.

This is your cosmic reporter now out and standing by.

Dr. King received confirmation and further details the next day from Adept Nixies Zero Zero Nine – Operation Earth Light is now officially fully operational.

Transmission #37
Monday, November 17th, 1990 – 12:00 Noon PST
Rest area 30 miles from Barstow, California
With Adept Nixies Zero Zero Six

Dr. King: Today is the 17th of November, 1990.

This is communication flash.

An official communique will be given to me possibly today at a later time. My position now is in a rest area approximately 30 miles from Barstow, California.

The information flash is this:

Tomorrow, on the 18th of November, the three units activated in Operation Earth Light will be deactivated for the time being.

End of intelligence report.

Seven days after the start of the first phase of Operation Earth Light the equipment was closed down, marking the completion of phase number 1. It was ironic that this information came through while Dr. King and I had just pulled off the interstate highway on our way back to Los Angeles from Lake Powell. We had stopped at a small rest stop for a short break. There, amidst dozens of cars and trucks and people milling around, Dr. King wandered away from the crowd with his hand-held tape recorder and recorded the above short yet historic communique.

History had been made – announced at a rest stop outside of Barstow, California.

Another vital step along the golden path towards the New Age had been taken. There were no headlines, no special interviews on network television, no celebrations to be seen. Mankind continued with their lives as though nothing had changed. Yet the evolved Masters of the Great White Brotherhood had started another mission on mankind's behalf. Another mission to raise as many upon earth as possible in time for the great change due to manifest on the Goddess Earth. A mission greatly enhanced due to its original design by a Master in an earth physical body – Dr. George King.

THE PHASES CONTINUE

Within weeks phase 2 of Operation Earth Light took place. Dr. King had learned that a phase would be commencing on December 24th with all seven units activated. A few days following the completion, Dr. King received the formal announcement of the phase.

Operation Earth Light – Phase 2

Transmission #38
Monday, December 29th, 1990 – 11:15 a.m. PST
Los Angeles, California
With Adept Nixies Zero Zero Nine

Dr. King: The date is December 29th, 1990. My position is Los Angeles. The time is 11:15 am PST.

I am waiting for a mental transmission from Adept Nixies Zero Zero Nine regarding the latest activation of Operation Earth Light.

Yes, Nixies Zero Zero Nine?

Adept Nixies Zero Zero Nine: The latest phases of Operation Earth Light on December 24th, 25th, and 26th went off very successfully indeed, without any hitches. But there was a lack of presence we all felt. That was the presence of your good self. You would have really enjoyed the complex manipulations

121

which went on during this time.

On behalf of the Spiritual Hierarchy of Earth, I convey our congratulations to you who originally designed this equipment so many years ago.

Well done, my friend.

This is Nixies Zero Zero Nine now out.

To many the situation was sad. Dr. King had spent a lifetime working to improve mankind's karmic position for the coming golden age. Yet now, as one of his missions was getting off the ground, he was unable to be where the action was. Adept Nixies Zero Zero Nine expressed the congratulations of all involved and stated that his presence was missed during this phase. They all knew how much Operation Earth Light meant to Dr. King and how much he would have enjoyed the manipulations that took place. Dr. King had proved through the years to be an expert on complex manipulation through his different world missions designed to help mankind.

As the words of Adept Nixies Zero Zero Nine sunk in, Dr. King's emotions got the better of him and he was unable to answer back, so the communication closed without his normal sign off. However, his emotion was not sadness. Instead, he was overcome with a type of shy joyousness. He was happy and proud that his mission was being performed and that his efforts were so worthy of appreciation by such evolved Masters.

Operation Earth Light – Phase 3

Transmission #39
Friday, April 5th, 1991 - 5:30 p.m. PST
Santa Barbara, California
With Adept Nixies Zero Zero Nine

Dr. King: Yes, Nixies Zero Zero Nine.

Adept Nixies Zero Zero Nine: At exactly 6:00 p.m. PST, three units of Operation Earth Light will go on the air and remain on the air for 24 hours. We must thank you for this wonderful mission.

Dr. King: This is Dr. King to Nixies Zero Zero Nine. I have picked that up. Thank you very much for the information. May this be released?

Adept Nixies Zero Zero Nine: Yes, it may, after the termination of this particular phase.

Dr. King: Thank you, Nixies Zero Zero Nine.

Adept Nixies Zero Zero Nine: This is Nixies Zero Zero Nine now out.

Dr. King: Dr. King now out – standing by for any further communication.

Transmission #40
Saturday, April 6th, 1991 – 6:05 p.m. PST
Santa Barbara, California
With Adept Nixies Zero Zero Five

Dr. King: It is Saturday, April 6th, 1991, at approximately 6:05 p.m. PST.

Yes, Nixies Zero Zero Five.

Adept Nixies Zero Zero Five: There has been a little holdup. Nixies Zero Zero Nine will contact you in few minutes for a release of information.

Dr. King: Thank you very much, Nixies Zero Zero Five. I deeply appreciate that.

Dr. King now out and standing by.

Adept Nixies Zero Zero Five: Nixies Zero Zero Five now out, standing by.

Dr. King was anxiously awaiting the communication from Adept Nixies Zero Zero Nine announcing the end of the current phase of Operation Earth Light. However, he learned later that it takes 15 minutes to properly close down the mission, which extends all over the world. The formal announcement cannot take place until this full close-down. Adept Nixies Zero Zero Five came through to inform him that there would be a short delay. This Adept, knowing Dr. King very well, realized that he would be getting quite anxious at even a short delay of 15 minutes.

Transmission #41
Saturday, April 6th, 1991 – 6:15 p.m. PST
Santa Barbara, California
With Adept Nixies Zero Zero Nine

Dr. King: Saturday, April 6th, 1991, approximately 6:15 p.m.

This is Dr. King. Yes, Nixies Zero Zero Nine.

Adept Nixies Zero Zero Nine: Operation Earth Light went very successfully.

Dr. King: Yes, Nixies Zero Zero Nine. May I now release this information.

Adept Nixies Zero Zero Nine: You may.

Dr. King: Thank you very much indeed.

Adept Nixies Zero Zero Nine: We have to thank and praise you.

This is Nixies Zero Zero Nine now out.

Dr. King: This is Dr. King now out.

Dr. King was very interested in reporting the Earth Light phases to his members and subscribers through his magazine *Cosmic Voice*. However, the actual recorded tape of the above message showed that he was very much affected by this report as well. His voice was starting to break up with emotion with his sign-off to Nixies Zero Zero Nine. Dr. King was a shy man, and the reminders through such transmissions of how important his Earth Light equipment had turned out to be was difficult for him to continue to hear in his frail health condition. This was a major factor why Dr. King requested, shortly after this phase, that he not be informed of future Operation Earth Light phases. Another reason was that he became very involved mentally with the phases when he knew about them. This was a notable trait of Dr. King with all of the missions that he was associated with throughout the years, and this was an important reason why his world missions were so successful. However, at this stage in his life, when his health was not what it used to be, he could not afford to focus on Operation Earth Light. He knew he needed to focus his attention on setting up his other missions properly so that The Aetherius Society could continue them after his passing on from earth.

Dr. King was satisfied that his design for Operation Earth Light had been manifested and that the mission was being performed correctly. He had every confidence that the Great White Brotherhood would continue the mission and perform it in an excellent and karmically correct manner. He could now detach himself from Operation Earth Light and turn his attention to other duties which only he could perform prior to his passing.

Known Phases of Operation Earth Light

Phase 1   November 11th — November 18th, 1990
              3 Units   7 days

Phase 2   December 24th — December 26th, 1990
              7 Units   2 days

Phase 3   April 5th — April 6th, 1991
              3 Units   1 day

Phase 4   September 29th — October 2nd, 1991
              7 Units   3 days

Phase 5   November 21st — November 22nd, 1991
              7 Units   1 day

The last two phases reported to Dr. King came through quickly with little communication. After phase 5, though the mission continued, the Masters respected Dr. King's wishes and did not report them to him.

CHAPTER 12

KARMIC HEALING

Operation Earth Light continues. We have glimpsed into the world of the Masters to witness the birth of a new and essential mission for our world. The energy from Operation Earth Light is helping usher in the New Age little by little. The vibrations upon earth are rising each day, bringing evolution as well as anxious unrest and change. Many on earth are not ready – but evolution must continue. The tensions will build as we approach the great change. There will be many who will not be able to withstand the vibrations of the New Age, even with all the help that is being provided. The Cosmic Masters state that through a slow, natural process, such life streams will be re-born on another, less evolved planet to continue their evolution.

The door to the New Age on earth is wide open but will not always be so. It is up to all of us to prepare ourselves and our fellow humans to enter through this door before it closes. The rewards will be magnificent. The speed of evolution in the New Age will be like nothing we have ever experienced. We will accelerate through our karma as never before, learn and evolve in a golden age conducive to spiritual growth.

But how can we all help build and prepare this dawning age of enlightenment?

The guidance given to mankind throughout the ages is

an important and essential foundation. This can be summed up as follows:

1. Follow the moral and ethical laws as taught by the major religions.

2. Raise our vibrations through the study of religious teachings and spiritual practices.

3. Help raise those around us through healing and prayer.

These activities have been and always will be essential to our evolution. Yet the days in which we now live are extraordinary and call for extraordinary actions.

The Masters realize this and are doing everything they can to help – yet their hands are partly tied due to mankind's karmic pattern.

We all must do our part. If we can improve mankind's karma we can enable the Masters to help us more as well as greatly improve the conditions on earth. This will allow more and more people to focus on the important aspects of life, which are the spiritual aspects of life.

Mankind's karma is in dire need of help. We have demonstrated selfishness throughout our history, destroying a planet on which we lived, plus two subsequent civilizations on earth. We have continued to war amongst ourselves throughout our history.

How can we heal our ailing karmic pattern?

The answer is karmic healing.

Karma is a pressure to evolve back to God. The more we can demonstrate that we are evolving as a race, the more karmic pressure will be relieved. The more we act like evolved beings, the more pressure is released from our self-made karmic "pressure cooker."

If those who are starting to realize their own divinity

focus less on their own development and more on helping others, they will demonstrate the vital wisdom of selflessness or, in other words, Oneness.

This will reflect not only on each individual's karmic pattern but on our civilization's as well.

"Man dwelleth in a world of selfishness – God dwelleth in a world of selfless expansion. Bridge this gap – and be a God."

> —*The Master Jesus, The Seventh Blessing.*
> *Sept. 7th, 1958* [18]

Individual development is important but should be secondary to world healing. In Dr. King's organization, The Aetherius Society, members have access to some of the most advanced spiritual practices on earth, yet Dr. King always emphasized the support and performance of the world missions. These missions, such as Operation Prayer Power, Operation Sunbeam, and The Saturn Mission are virtually healing the karma of mankind in a most potent manner. Such world healing is imperative for the New Age to dawn on earth. It is time for all spiritually minded people to come together and throw their all into working for world peace. More and more individuals and spiritual groups around the world are starting to realize this. The new millennium and recent planetary configurations sparked several successful calls for synchronized global prayers, and the trend is continuing.

One excellent set of prayers everyone can use to help heal the karma of the world is contained in *The Twelve Blessings*. The Master Jesus gave this mystic set of prayers and blessings to earth especially for these days. This short yet powerful ritual begins by directing spiritual energy out to our world. However, it then goes beyond this and directs our love and blessings to such evolved Beings as the Mother Earth, the mighty Sun, and even the Galaxy itself. By sending our thanks to such Beings we demonstrate our realization of our place in Creation and give thanks to those who help us in our journey back to God. Through the law of karma, a stream of energy returns back from these Beings to the person praying, and, as we are representing mankind, a stream of energy is also returned back to mankind as a whole. This is a very powerful and uplifting karmic healing practice, which must be practiced in order to appreciate its power.

Let us also remember the much-needed practical forms of service. Organizations such as the Red Cross, Doctors without Borders, and the dozens of other charitable organizations dedicated to helping those in need are excellent ways anyone can help heal and uplift our civilization. These organizations do a tremendous amount of good, both for those they help directly as well as all those who observe through the media and learn from their examples the benefit of helping others.

This also is karmic healing.

This is Service.

"This is the great key, the great yoga, the great practice, the great Christianity, the great religion. The greatest deeds that you can do in these days.

"Service, Service, Service – is the key which opens the doors to all powers, to all forms of enlightenment – service to others."

—*The Master Aetherius, You Choose. Feb. 28th, 1960* [19]

The Masters are doing their part through Operation Earth Light and many other ways. It is up to all of us to respond to the needs of the day and do our part. To demonstrate that mankind is ready for the New Age. To demonstrate that we fully realize we are all One – that we really are our brother's keeper. To actively help as many enter the

New Age as possible.

Those who have been doing this know full well what it brings – a feeling of joy beyond all joys. A knowledge from deep within you rises as you know you are doing your part to help mankind in these important times.

"Transmute selfishness into SERVICE for others and your reward will come. Enlightenment, like the break of dawn upon the darkest night, will cast the shadows of this night before it...

"Serve and the mighty power of kundalini will rise in unforced fashion and open the chakra jewels in your higher bodies."

—*Mars Sector 6, The Third Freedom. Feb. 22nd, 1961* [20]

NOTES

1. This great event was recorded and published in the book, *The Day The Gods Came* by George King, D.D. The Aetherius Society, 1965.

2. For a more detailed description of the Cosmic Concept as given by the advanced Masters see *The Nine Freedoms* by George King, D.D. The Aetherius Society, 1963.

3. For a complete description and directions to the 19 holy mountains see *The Holy Mountains of the World* edited by Charles Abrahamson. The Aetherius Society, 1994.

4. *Dark Matter, Missing Planets and New Comets* by Tom Van Flandern. North Atlantic Books, 1993.

5. For further information on the spiritual practices taught by Dr. King read *Realize Your Inner Potential* by George King D.D., and Richard Lawrence, D.D. 1998.

6. For a complete description and directions to the 19 holy mountains see *The Holy Mountains of the World* edited by Charles Abrahamson. The Aetherius Society, 1994

7. For details of some of the results of Operation Prayer Power, contact The Aetherius Society for back issues of *Cosmic Voice*.

8. For further information on Operation Bluewater see *Contact with the Gods From Space* by George King, D.D., Richard Lawrence, D.D. 1996 and selected issues of *Cosmic Voice* available from The Aetherius Society.

9. *Visit to the Logos of Earth* by George King, D.D. The Aetherius Society, 1986.

10. From *Visit to the Logos of Earth* by George King,

D.D. The Aetherius Society, 1986.

11. *The Nine Freedoms* by George King, D.D. The Aetherius Society, 1963.

12. For more information on Dr. King's initiation into a mystical order of the Spiritual Hierarchy of Earth see *Operation Sunbeam – God's Magic in Action* by George King, D.D. The Aetherius Society, 1979.

13. The kundalini is the primordial force within the body which animates it and makes all functions possible. It normally lies semi-dormant in the chakra at the base of the spine. When fully activated and risen through the channel called Sushumna within the spine it opens and energizes the chakras so that their full potential may be realized.

14. *My Contact with the Great White Brotherhood* by George King, D.D. The Aetherius Society, 1962.

15. The Tactical Team is a group of dedicated members of The Aetherius Society who have proved their dedication through years of service in The Aetherius Society. They are entrusted with the performing of the world missions such as Operation Sunbeam and The Saturn Mission.

16. *Visit to the Logos of Earth* by George King, D.D. The Aetherius Society, 1986.

17. *Cosmic Voice* Volume 11, Issues 20 & 21. The Aetherius Society, 1990

18. *The Twelve Blessings* by George King, D.D. The Aetherius Society, 1958.

19. *Cosmic Voice* Issue 25, The Aetherius Society, 1962.

20. *The Nine Freedoms* by George King, D.D. The Aetherius Society, 1963.

BIBLIOGRAPHY

Abrahamson, Charles
The Holy Mountains of the World, The Aetherius Society, 1994

Boissiere, Robert
Meditations with The Hopi, Bear & Company, 1986

Hodson, Geoffrey
The Kingdom of the Gods,
The Theosophical Publishing House, 1952

King, D.D. Th.D., George
Contact Your Higher Self Through Yoga, 1955

Cosmic Voice, Volume No. 1, 1957

Cosmic Voice, Volume No. 2, 1957

The Twelve Blessings, 1958

Cosmic Voice, Issue 25, 1962

My Contact with the Great White Brotherhood, 1962

The Nine Freedoms, 1963

The Day The Gods Came, 1965

The Five Temples of God, 1967

You Too Can Heal, 1976

Operation Sunbeam – God's Magic in Action, 1979

Karma and Reincarnation, 1986

Visit to the Logos of Earth, 1986

Contact with a Lord of Karma, 1989

Cosmic Voice, Volume 11, Issues 20 & 21

Cassettes
The Spirit Realms, 1973

Karma and Reincarnation, 1974

The Great White Brotherhood, 1974

Occult Revelations about a Psychic Center of Earth, 1977

Concentration, Contemplation and Meditation, 1977

The Cosmic Plan, 1978

The Realms of the Masters, 1978

The Devic Kingdom, 1978

Life After Death, 1982

King, D.D., Th.D., George with Dr. Richard Lawrence, D.D.
Contact with the Gods from Space, The Aetherius Society, 1996

Realize Your Inner Potential, The Aetherius Society, 1998

Leadbeater, Charles
The Inner Life, The Theosophical Publishing House, 1978

Lorler, Marie-Lu
Shamanic Healing, Brotherhood of Life, 1989

Mann, A. T.
Millennium Prophecies, Element Books, 1992

Sivananda, Swami
The Bhagavad Gita, Divine Life Society, 1939

Skinner, Stephen
Millennium Prophecies, Virgin Books, 1994

Van Flandern, Tom
Dark Matter, Missing Planets and New Comets,
North Atlantic Books, 1993

Van Gelder, Dora
The Real World of Fairies ,
The Theosophical Publishing House, 1977

Waters, Frank
Book of the Hopi, Ballantine Books, 1963

INDEX

The Aetherius Press

LOS ANGELES • FOUNDED 1955 • LONDON

NEW AGE & METAPHYSICAL BOOK PUBLISHERS

For further information about The Aetherius Society
and the karmic missions of Dr. George King, please contact:

The Aetherius Society
American Headquarters
6202 Afton Place
Los Angeles, CA 90028
U.S.A.
Tel. 1-(800)800-1354

The Aetherius Society
European Headquarters
757 Fulham Road
London SW6 5UU
U.K.
Tel. (0171) 736-4187

Or visit our website at
www.aetherius.org